RANK & FILE

RANK
&
FILE

Grange
BOOKS

First published in 2000 as
Swinging The Lead and Spiking His Guns

This edition published by Grange Books in 2003
Reprinted in 2004

an imprint of Grange Books PLC
The Grange
Kingsnorth Industrial Estate
Hoo nr Rochester
Kent
UK
ME3 9ND
www.grangebooks.co.uk

Typeset by David Onyett, Publishing & Production Services,
Cheltenham
Printed in Thailand for Imago Publishing

INTRODUCTION

Just as English history has been influenced by battles and wars down the ages, the English language also reflects the impact of warfare in the many words and expressions that it has inherited from our military and naval past. The great majority of these have shed their earlier associations, whether they first saw action on the medieval battlefield, aboard an eighteenth-century man-of-war, or on the Western Front. Today they have found a fresh identity and purpose in modern usage that often obscures their fascinating origin and development.

Swinging The Lead and Spiking His Guns explores the history of hundreds of words and phrases which started out in the working language of soldiers, sailors, knights and airmen before finding their way into everyday speech. The book unearths many intriguing and unexpected associations: how the 'bikini' came to be named after a Pacific island; why 'sabotage' owes a debt to the footwear of French peasants; and what a swordsman had to do in order to become a 'swashbuckler'.

The wide range of words and turns of phrase covered by the book also reveals in miniature something of the history of the British people at home and abroad. From the Roman occupation of Britain, which introduced the Latin vocabulary of the Roman army, to the global extent of the British Empire itself, English has borrowed, adapted and been influenced by the languages of enemies and allies the world over.

French, brought to England by Norman conquerors in the eleventh century, had a profound influence on the development and expansion of military terms and phrases in English; as it has done in every other branch of our linguistic heritage. Other European languages, including Dutch, German, Italian and Swedish have made lasting contributions as well.

Further afield, Arabic words lie at the root of familiar English ones such as 'admiral', 'arsenal' and 'magazine'. The British occupation of India left a lasting linguistic legacy in the British army, of which the 'dum-dum' bullet, the 'tank' and 'khaki' are just three examples. Elsewhere in the book you will find one of the very few English words borrowed from the language of Polynesia. Wherever they sailed, fought and settled, English-speakers eagerly acquired local words, changed them as they thought fit and brought them home.

Time has been no barrier either in the steady evolution and growth of our vocabulary. The Trojan war may be a legend when related by Homer in the *Iliad*, but this has not prevented it from providing English with expressions that are still current today when people 'hector' one another in 'stentorian' voices, perhaps discovering someone's 'Achilles heel' in the process.

Famous figures from recorded military history have played their part as well. Julius Caesar's crossing of the Rubicon in 49 B.C. and his victory at Zela two years later have left their mark on English. From more recent times the Duke of Wellington is perhaps as well remembered today for the waterproof boots bearing his name, as he is for his defeat of Napoleon at the Battle of Waterloo in 1815.

Then there are those once famous individuals who have disappeared from most history books, but whose names are recalled in words and phrases which still survive: Pyrrhus, King of Epirus, and Lord Raglan have much to thank the English language for in helping to preserve their names in our collective usage, if not our memory.

English is one of the world's richest and most versatile languages; how many, for instance, could form an association between a scarecrow and a shell which fails to detonate? In this selection words and expressions from ancient times sit happily alongside others coined within the last century. Only a small proportion can be examined here, but they act as an indication of the diverse legacy from which our language has grown and continues to grow.

Achilles heel

Achilles, the great Greek hero of the Trojan wars and the slayer of the Trojan hero, Hector, was invincible except for one weak spot – his heel. According to legend, Achilles' mother Thetis dipped her son in the river Styx to make him invulnerable. In doing this, she held him by one heel and that heel remained dry and therefore unprotected. Achilles fought many battles from which he emerged unscathed; it was only an arrow which struck him in the heel his mother had held that finally slew him. Since then an 'Achilles heel' has referred to a 'weak spot' of any sort. By association, the tendon which connects the heel and the calf in the human leg is called the Achilles tendon.

Admiral

With a powerful naval tradition peopled by national heroes like Sir Francis Drake and Horatio Nelson, our image of an 'admiral' is so quintessentially British that it comes as a surprise to discover that the word 'admiral' is Arabic in origin. The Muslim rank *amir* (a high commander) is familiar today in titles such as Emir and this is where the English word 'admiral' finds its root. In Arabic an *amir al bar* was a 'commander of the sea'.

Alarm

The warning sound giving notice of danger was originally a call to arms: a warning to seize weapons and man the defences at times of attack. The modern English 'alarm' stems from the Italian *allarme*, or *all' arme*, meaning 'to the arms'. In Middle English this was adopted as 'alarme', which, by the fourteenth century had become 'alarm'. At one time 'alarum' was used in all senses to mean 'alarm', but this has gradually become restricted to describe the note of a warning bell or clock.

Alert

'Alert' is another military expression that owes its origin to Italian usage. In this instance the Italian term is *all' erte*, in which *all'* is again an abbreviation of *alla* (meaning 'to the') and *erta* ('look-out' [tower]). Those who were stationed on look-out duty, whether in specially constructed towers or not, were expected to be 'alert' at all times.

All Sir Garnet

This expression recalls the career and exploits of the Victorian military commander, Sir Garnet Wolseley. Entering the service in 1852, he saw action in a number of campaigns: Burma, the Crimea, the Indian Mutiny, the Red River rebellion in Canada, the Ashanti war in West Africa, South Africa and Egypt. As commander of the Sudan expedition to relieve General Gordon in Khartoum in 1884, he reached the pinnacle of his logistical and tactical expertise. Although his forces arrived too late to save Gordon, the organization and subsequent success of the campaign was widely regarded as a significant military and personal triumph. From 1890 to 1895 Sir Garnet Wolseley was commander-in-chief of the entire British army. Throughout his career the confidence his reputation spread throughout the army assured all the troops under his command that everything was under control and as it should be. So the expression 'All Sir Garnet' became a general confirmation that everything is well in hand.

Ally

'Ally' is used as both a verb and a noun. In the former sense it means to 'join' an individual or group as an associate or confederate; in the latter 'ally' refers to a 'kinsman' or one who is joined to another through a mutual cause. Both stem from the French *allier*, which itself is rooted in the old French word, *aleier*, that was used to describe the process by which metals were fused to form an 'alloy'.

Aloof

The influence of Britain's naval heritage is seen in many expressions that have entered the language in general. Aboard a sailing ship, 'aloof' referred to a specific order given to the helmsman, requiring him to steer the ship closer to the windward quarter, or 'luff', thereby keeping the ship well away from a hazard, or dangerous shoreline, towards which it was being blown. In its broader, and now more familiar context, 'aloof' means staying clear of someone or something of which one is unsure and a little suspicious.

Ambulance

The ambulance is one of the more humane developments in the history of warfare, coming down to us from Baron Dominique Jean Larrey, personal surgeon to Napoleon Bonaparte two centuries ago. It was he who developed the specially designed covered litter for transporting wounded men from the field of battle, which replaced the rough, unsprung carts that had been used until then. In 1792 Larrey's first ambulance went into service, providing a well-sprung vehicle, equipped with bandages and first-aid equipment, for the greater comfort and well-being of Napoleon's wounded troops. Ambulances like these were first used in the Italian campaign of 1796–7, in which they acquired the French name *ambulance*, replacing the earlier expression *hôpital ambulant* (meaning 'a walking hospital').

Andrew Millar

The Napoleonic wars also provided the Royal Navy with this unusual nickname. Some associations link 'Andrew Millar' with a company supplying the fleet with provisions. But 'Andrew Millar's regiment', or just 'the Andrew', is generally taken to be a reference to the activities of one Andrew Millar, the leader of a notorious press-gang in the Portsmouth area. So ruthless and, no-doubt, effective, were his methods of acquiring 'recruits', that before long his victims were described as having been snatched into 'the Andrew'.

Armada

In the history of England reference to an 'armada' invariably brings to mind the Spanish Armada: the large invasion fleet sent against England in July 1588 by Philip II of Spain, which was defeated in a series of running battles in the Channel by the far smaller English navy commanded by Lord Howard of Effingham. However, the word 'armada' originated in Latin, where *armata* means 'equipped with arms'. In time the word *armado* developed in Spanish and by the sixteenth century had come to refer to a fleet of warships.

Army

As an armed force, an 'army' takes its origins from the same Latin root as 'armada'. The Latin verb *armare*, means to equip with weapons (*arma* in Latin). In Old French this developed into *armée*, the word used to describe a force that had been armed with weapons and by the fourteenth century Geoffrey Chaucer was using 'army' as the name for such a force in English.

Arsenal

The name of one of London's most successful football clubs follows a historical trail that takes it back to the Muslim world, by way of Woolwich and Venice. The first place to be called anything resembling the English word 'arsenal' was a dockyard area of Venice known as the *Arsenale*. This was derived from a local word *arzana*, which came in turn from the Arabic *dar-accina'ah*, meaning 'a house of mechanical industry'. In due course the industry in question became the making of armaments. In England, the Royal Arsenal was sited at Woolwich at the end of the seventeenth century. Prior to that Henry VIII had created the Royal Dockyard at Woolwich in 1512, giving this 'arsenal' an earlier maritime connection, like that in Venice. The Woolwich Arsenal Football Club was founded in 1886 and the Arsenal team is still nicknamed 'the Gunners' in spite of having moved to Highbury in 1913.

At full tilt

In jousting, combatants riding against each other with lances were separated by a barrier known as a 'tilt'. In time 'tilt' came to refer to the combat itself and, by extension, a joust undertaken 'at full tilt' was an all-out contest taken at the gallop in which nothing was spared in speed or ferocity. The expression that has come down from medieval combat still carries a sense of forceful, unbending purpose. So an enterprise undertaken 'at full tilt' is conducted with maximum speed and endeavour.

At the eleventh hour

Although the last of the labourers hired in the parable of the labourers in St Matthew's gospel were hired 'at the eleventh hour', the phrase has taken on a distinctly martial tone since the signing of the armistice at the eleventh hour of the eleventh day of the eleventh month of 1918, which ended the First World War. In its biblical, and more usual, sense, 'at the eleventh hour' has become synonymous with 'at the last minute'.

AWOL

The term 'absent without leave' is these days applied to any period of unofficial absenteeism and is usually referred to by its acronym 'awol'. This is a comparatively recent development in the evolution of an expression which was first used during the American Civil War, when offenders were made to wear a sign bearing the initials 'A.W.O.L.' The 'O' was intended to make it clear that the offender had not been 'absent *with* leave'. The term was soon adopted by the British army, though during the First World War the initials were still pronounced individually. Only after the Second World War did their pronunciation as an acronym become widespread.

Backs to the wall

In moments of desperation, when there is no option other than making a final stand, you can be said to have your 'back to the wall'. The image is graphic and conveys something of the desperate hand-to-hand combat in which a beleaguered combatant places himself with his back against a wall to prevent attack from the rear. In doing this, however, he also cuts himself off from any further retreat. The term was taken up by Earl Haig in 1918, when he issued his famous order to British troops on 12 April. In the face of what turned out to be the final German offensive of the First World War, he commanded that 'Every position must be held to the last man: there must be no retirement. With our backs to the wall, and believing in the justice of our cause, each one of us must fight on to the end.'

Backroom boys

This widely-used nickname for scientists and technicians was first given a public airing by Lord Beaverbrook, British minister for aircraft production in the Second World War. Paying tribute to the members of his department who invented the new instruments and weapons which kept the RAF one step ahead of the Luftwaffe for most of the war, in a speech broadcast on 19 March 1941, he told his listeners, 'Let me say that the credit belongs to the boys in the backrooms. It isn't the man who sits in the limelight who should have the praise. It is not the men who sit in prominent places. It is the men in the backrooms.'

Balaclava helmet

The bitter winter weather experienced by British troops fighting in the Crimean War of 1854–6, led to much improvisation to keep warm. One of the more successful innovations was a knitted woollen hood, which fitted like a helmet over the wearer's head and neck, with only a hole for the face. This design has been copied to produce wetsuit headgear for divers and ski-masks for winter sports enthusiasts. But the knitted garment still bears the name of the inconclusive military campaign waged around the town of Balaclava, made famous by the gallant but ill-timed Charge of the Light Brigade on 25 October 1854.

The balloon's gone up

The start of excitement or action is vividly encapsulated in this phrase which dates from the First World War, when often the first sign of an atack beginning was the launching of a balloon. These could be signal balloons, commanding gunners along the front to begin firing, or balloons carrying aloft observers to direct an advance. Either way, to the troops in the trenches, word that 'the balloon's gone up' meant that action of some form was imminent.

Barbarians

The uncivilized and uncouth have been called 'barbarians' ever since the ancient Greeks took to calling anyone who spoke a foreign language 'babblers' (*barbaros*): those who spoke a language they did not understand. From the Greek word, came the Latin *barbaricus*, leading to the English 'barbarian'. In its ancient usage, the word did not carry particular warlike or savage overtones; these were added as the ancient civilizations fell to the barbarian hordes that finally overwhelmed them.

Barricade

'Barricades', hastily thrown up defences used to block a street or building from attack, first entered the language (in this case French) in Paris, in 1588. In defiance of the hated king, Henry III, his adversary Henri de Guise returned to the city. The king called out his Swiss Guards in the face of whom the Parisians threw chains across the street, tore up the paving stones and erected barriers made from barrels (*barriques* in French) filled with earth and stones, from behind which they shot down the king's troops. This action led to the king being forced from his capital and 12 May has been known as *La journée des barricades* ('the day of the barricades') ever since. The erection of barricades in Paris occurred on several occasions during the following centuries, leading in part to Napoleon III's street-widening scheme in the middle of the nineteenth century; not that this prevented the Communards from successfully erecting their barriers during the second siege of Paris in 1871.

Bastion

By the sixteenth century 'bastion' was well established in English to describe a projecting part of a fortification. This developed from earlier French military terminology, in which a *bastillon* was a 'fortress', that gave the name to the Bastille, the celebrated fortress used as a state prison in Paris, which was singled out for attack by the mob on 14 July 1789 at the very start of the French Revolution. Troops fighting in a 'bastion' were given a far wider angle of fire than that provided by a castle's battlements. In time 'bastion' was applied to a fortress itself and by association acquired its metaphorical meaning as a stronghold.

Battering-ram

Before the use of gunpowder in warfare, the 'battering-ram' had been one of the principal siege weapons dating back to biblical times. Although it was later refined in its design, the 'battering-ram' was essentially a heavy beam that was swung against defensive gates or walls until they were weakened or broken down. It was common for 'battering-rams' to be capped with a heavy iron weight at the striking end. This was often shaped in the form of a ram's head, no doubt in recognition of that animal's habit of head-butting opponents. The analogy was so well-observed in the Roman world that the Latin for a 'battering-ram' is *aries*, the noun for a male sheep (or ram) and the name of the constellation symbolized by a ram.

Battery

'Battery' is a word that has evolved in meaning as technology has developed. At its root is the Latin verb *battuere* meaning 'to strike' and 'to beat' from which derived the French *batterie*, the military term for an artillery 'battery' (a group of guns placed together to operate as a unit). This meaning of 'battery' was current in English by the sixteenth century. However, a fresh meaning was acquired in the mid-eighteenth century following the discovery of a means of storing an electric current. This breakthrough was made in the Dutch university of Leyden, where glass jars lined inside and out with tinfoil were found to hold an electric charge. A group of these Leyden jars placed together presumably resembled a group of cannons in appearance, and the term 'battery' began to be applied in English to all devices that stored electricity.

Battleaxe

A formidable woman (usually elderly) can be unflatteringly referred to as a 'battleaxe', particularly when she makes her views known in forthright manner. The term became associated with outspoken women when the early American movement for women's rights began to publish a journal called *The Battle Axe*. The weapon itself was a sharp, broad axe. Used by Gothic tribes, it was capable of piercing Roman armour and shields. In the hands of medieval knights, it was a deadly hacking weapon in the melée of battle.

Bayonet

In the seventeenth century 'bayonet' was the name given to a short dagger; a century later it had acquired the more specific application by which it is known today, as a stabbing instrument for fixing to the muzzle of a rifle. In both cases the 'bayonet' takes its name from the town of Bayonne, the site of its original manufacture and the *Tabourot Des Accords*, an account of trade at the time, dating from the close of the sixteenth century, refers to *bayonnettes de Bayonne*.

Bearing the brunt

To 'bear the brunt' of any action is to take the main impact, the greater part of the shock and stress. The term dates from the fourteenth century, a time when opposing forces in battle lined up against each other and those in the front line bore the greatest share of the enemy onslaught. By extension, the 'brunt of the battle' is the 'hottest' part of the fighting, which may imply an association with the earlier Nordic word *bruna*, meaning 'to advance like fire'. (The English word 'burn' stems from the same source and is an example of the process of metathesis, the transposition of letters, which formed part of the development of many words in use today.)

Bellicose

An adjective meaning warlike, 'bellicose' is virtually a direct borrowing from the Latin adjective of the same meaning *bellicus*, which has its roots in *bellum*, the Latin noun for 'war'.

Berserk

Anyone described as 'berserk' is taken to be in a state of wild, reckless frenzy. This was the description given to the original 'berserkers': Viking warriors who either went into battle *bare* to the *sark* (shirt) or clad in a *bear sark*. In both cases their lack of armour showed their contempt for death and the need for frenzied fighting, if they were to survive.

Between the devil and the deep blue sea

Any impossible predicament can be described thus, but in naval parlance 'between the devil and the deep blue sea' had a particular meaning. The 'devil' referred to was a particularly inaccessible part of the ship's hull, either a seam at water-level, or a board attached to the hull to support the heavy guns run out above. In both cases reaching the 'devil' may have been hazardous, but it was unquestionably better than being lost in the 'deep blue sea'. Reference to the seam in the hull that required regular sealing to keep it watertight occurs in the expression 'the devil to pay and no hot pitch', which means trouble may be expected with no means of avoiding it.

Beware Greeks bearing gifts

As a warning against being deceived, this recalls the story of the Trojan horse which led to the downfall of the ancient city of Troy. After ten years of fighting, the besieging Greek army constructed a large wooden horse, filled it with armed men and then withdrew as if they were returning home. The Trojans were persuaded to drag the horse inside the city, having been tricked by a captive left behind by the Greeks, into believing that it was an offering to the goddess Athene which would render Troy impregnable. Once the horse was inside the city walls, the same wily captive released the warriors hidden in it, who overpowered the guards and opened the city gates to the main Greek force which had returned under cover of darkness.

Bikini

The military associations of this celebrated two-piece swimsuit may not be immediately apparent, until you consider the date of its first appearance: 5 July 1946. This was the day on which the new beach wear designed by French couturier Louis Reard first went on show at a fashion show in Paris. Five days earlier the United States had detonated the first atomic bomb at Bikini Atoll in the Pacific. The original name for Mr Reard's sensational creation was, not unnaturally, *le minimum*. However, this was rapidly eclipsed by 'bikini', a name that encapsulated the idea of ultimate devastation (for the male half of the population at any rate). It was reported at the time that Micheline Bernardi, the dancer who was shown in newspaper photographs reclining in the first bikini, received 50,000 fan letters.

Bint

British soldiers serving in India and the Middle East adopted a number of local words into their everyday language. Among these was the Arabic word *bint*, meaning a 'girl' or 'woman', which was widely used in the army to describe any girl or woman. It gradually fell from use after the Second World War, as the British army steadily withdrew from its overseas bases.

Biting the bullet

In the days before anaesthetics were available on the battlefield, the wounded had to be treated without painkillers. To brace themselves against the agony of their operations, patients were told to bite on the soft lead of a bullet, which would absorb the pressure of their bite without breaking their teeth. The expression has entered the language to describe preparing oneself for something unpleasant or painful.

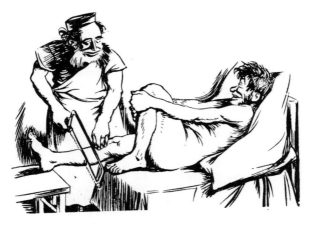

Bivouac

A 'bivouac' is an enforced stopping place, usually under some form of improvised shelter, when circumstances necessitate taking cover until the situation improves. In its original sense 'bivouac' was a 'night-watch under arms', from where the association with a temporary encampment without tents derived. In Switzerland a *beiwacht*, which is related to 'bivouac', was an 'extra watch' comprising citizens who joined the regular town watch on nightly patrols at times of danger.

Blarney

In 1602 Blarney Castle, near Cork in Ireland, was the scene of prolonged negotiations between one Cormac Macarthy and Queen Elizabeth I's Lord President. Macarthy had been ordered to surrender the castle as part of an armistice but he daily prevaricated, offering nothing more than reassuring statements to the Lord President that he was willing to comply with the Queen's wishes. However, his string of excuses prolonged the negotiations for so long that the Lord President became the laughing stock of the royal court and the Queen herself expressed her exasperation at yet 'more Blarney talk'. Since then deceptive flattery of all kinds has been termed 'Blarney', assisted no doubt by the legend of the Blarney stone set in the castle walls, which, once kissed, is said to endow the kisser ever after with a flattering tongue and the ability to lie shamelessly.

Blighty

'Blighty' is another word that found its way back to Great Britain thanks to British troops stationed in India. They adopted the Hindi word *bilayati*, meaning 'far away' or 'foreign', and gave it their own specific meaning of 'England' or 'home'. During the First World War 'Blighty' was used by troops from all parts of the British Empire to refer to 'home' wherever it happened to be.

Blimp

A 'blimp', based on David Low's cartoon character Colonel Blimp, is an elderly, dyed-in-the-wool reactionary, opposed to all and any change. Colonel Blimp came to prominence in the years following the First World War when the word 'blimp' was first used to describe a type of observation balloon. These were small, non-rigid, lighter-than-air airships. According to one line of thought there were two types: A-limp airships and B-limp airships. Tests proved the latter to be the better design and the B-limp airship was taken into service, rapidly acquiring its less formal appellation 'blimp', possibly coined by the aviator Horace Scott. Another theory holds that 'blimp' was formed from 'blister' and 'lump', words that aptly described the balloon's appearance.

Blitz

The 'Blitz' became entrenched in the English language during the Second World War as the name given to the intensive German air raids launched against London in the second half of 1940. 'Blitz' was an abbreviated form of the German word *Blitzkrieg* ('lightning war'), which was a vivid description of the sudden, concentrated offensives on land and in the air, by which invading German forces were able to overwhelm and defeat defending armies in other European countries, notably Poland, Czechoslovakia, Norway, Belgium and the Netherlands.

Blockbuster

These days a 'blockbuster' is frequently associated with a huge show business success. Multimillion dollar films especially are referred to as blockbusters in anticipation of even greater returns at the box office. The term originated during the Second World War among RAF bomber crews, who gave the name 'blockbusters' to huge bombs they carried, capable of destroying whole groups of buildings or otherwise impenetrable enemy structures.

Boffin

Scientists engaged in creating new military equipment and techniques, were given the nickname 'boffins' by RAF crews during the Second World War. The name soon spread to the other armed services and from there entered civilian life. The origin of the word is obscure, although it may owe something to Charles Dickens, whose novel *Our Mutual Friend* includes an eccentric character named Mr Boffin.

Boondocks

The 'boondocks', or the back of beyond, came into general use through American troops serving in the Philippines during the Second World War. Those sent to the remote mountain regions took to referring to their postings as the 'boondocks', from the word for mountain, *bundok*, in the Philippine language Tagalog.

Booty

As the 'spoils of war', 'booty' has been known in English since the fifteenth century, when it was first recorded by Caxton. It originated from the German *büte*, meaning an 'exchange' or 'distribution' and these days refers to any form of prize or profit.

Broadside

Today's 'broadside', a vehement verbal onslaught, harks back to the days of naval gunnery, when the simultaneous firing of all the guns on one side of a ship was known as a 'broadside'.

Buccaneer

The first 'buccaneers' were specialists in curing meat; only later was the name given to pirates. Early in the seventeenth century, French and English hunters of pigs and wild cattle in the Caribbean adopted the local practice of curing the meat of their prey on a wooden framework called a *boucan*; similar to the structure called a *barbacoa*, from which the word 'barbecue' is derived. French hunters became known as *boucaniers* and the name was transferred to those who combined the use of the *boucan* with hunting down ships and treasure at sea.

Buckshee

'Buckshee' became part of military slang among British troops serving in India during the nineteenth century. Based on the Persian word *baksheesh*, which means a gratuity, the English version came to mean a tip, or something else given free. To receive something 'buckshee' implies getting it as a bonus, over and above what you were expecting or entitled to.

Bulldog breed

The British became known as the 'bulldog breed' during the second half of the nineteenth century; a popular music hall song of 1897 referred to men serving in the Royal Navy as 'boys of the bulldog breed'. At the outbreak of the First World War, in 1914, Winston Churchill was First Lord of the Admiralty. Speaking at a 'Call to Arms' meeting in London he drew a memorable comparison between the Royal Navy and a bulldog, striking a bulldog-like pose and expression as he made his point. During the Second World War, when Churchill was prime minister, model bulldogs went on sale bearing his face with its same defiant pout.

Burning your boats

The action of 'burning your boats' is an irrevocable step, from which there is no turning back. The image dates from military campaigns in the ancient world, when invaders who destroyed the vessels in which they had crossed rivers or arrived by sea, were left with no option but to defeat their foes or die.

Burying the hatchet

The hatchet was a key weapon of war among North American Indians. When conflicts had been settled, smoking the peace pipe was a signal that all weapons should be buried, so that all ideas of hostility would be hidden from sight. 'Burying the hatchet' today means letting bygones be bygones and ceasing to quarrel.

Buying a packet

This was one of several euphemisms for death among RAF crews in the Second World War. Airmen who failed to return from missions were said to have 'bought a packet', frequently reduced simple to 'bought it'. In the other services 'buying a packet' was also used to describe suffering a casualty.

Camouflage

The use of camouflage to disguise the appearance of someone or something dates from far back in military history, however it was in the twentieth century that it became an elaborate and sophisticated component of military strategy. The French verb *camoufler* means 'to disguise' and its noun *camouflage* described the often elaborate measures taken to hide military installations during the World Wars. Since then 'camouflage' has taken on a broader meaning with reference to any action designed to conceal or obscure.

Campaign

In military terms a 'campaign' is an army's operations in the field. This use dates back to the time when armies remained in quarters during the winter until the arrival of summer enabled them to move into the country (*campagna* in Italian and *campagne* in French). In English 'campaign' developed from its continental roots to become both a noun and a verb.

Canteen

Today a 'canteen' can be used to describe a number of elements connected with eating and drinking. There are 'canteens' of cutlery: boxes or cases fitted with compartments for housing knives, forks and spoons. 'Canteens' are also refreshment rooms serving food and drink in factories, hospitals, schools and anywhere else in which large numbers of people need to be fed swiftly and efficiently. Personal water bottles and mess-tins, particularly those used by soldiers, are called 'canteens' as well. In military camps and bases the 'canteen' is also the liquor shop. This last meaning is a direct descendant of the earliest use of 'canteen' in a military context. In Italian a *cantina* is a cellar and it was in cellars serving wine that soldiers used to gather to drink. When the 'canteen' moved out of the cellar, the use of the name widened to include somewhere where food was served, as well as a cutler's shop in camp. Outside camp, 'canteens' became portable stalls from which food and drink could be obtained.

Cardigan

The knitted woollen jacket that buttons down the front is one of several garments that came into being during the Crimean War of 1854–6. Faced with the biting cold of the Russian winter, British troops improvised a number of items of clothing in an attempt to keep themselves warm. Such garments were not restricted to the ordinary troops; officers also took to wearing knitted jackets under their uniforms and greatcoats. One of these was the Earl of Cardigan, commander of the Light Brigade, who led the fatal charge against Russian guns, which decimated his force at the Battle of Balaclava on 25 October 1854. In spite of this, he returned home to a hero's welcome and the 'cardigan' was duly named after him.

Carte blanche

In French a *carte blanche* literally means a 'blank paper' and the term was originally used in a military context at times of unconditional surrender. The defeated force would issue a blank paper, on which their victors could write their own terms and conditions, knowing that they would be accepted. Today the term is used in a figurative sense, conferring complete freedom of action on whoever has been given 'carte blanche'.

Cartridge

Cartridges today can be convenient containers of ink and film as well as ammunition for firearms. However, it was in this latter sense that the 'cartridge' first came into being in English, by way of French and Italian. When gunpowder arrived in medieval Europe from the Middle East and China, it was a valuable commodity which needed to be carefully measured and stored. *Carta*, a type of thick paper developed in Italy, was used to wrap a small charge of gunpowder in what soon became known as a *cartoccio*. This passed into French as a *cartouche* and into English as a *cartridge*. Later in its evolution, bullets or shot were added to cartridges as the technology of loading and firing guns advanced.

Catapult

'Catapult', used as both a noun and a verb, originated from the Greek *katapeltes* formed from the words for 'down' and 'hurl'.

Catapults were used throughout the ancient world (the Romans called their version *catapulta*) and though they varied in design, they all performed the basic function of hurling stones, arrows or other missiles. In the nineteenth century a forked stick fitted with an elastic band became popularly known as a hand-held 'catapult'. In the twentieth century catapult as a verb meaning 'to hurl' or 'forcefully launch' came into use.

Catch–22

The American novelist Joseph Heller takes the credit for originating the expression 'Catch–22'. Heller used it as the title of his 1955 novel about Captain Yossarian, an American airman serving with a bomber squadron in Europe, whose principal occupation is avoiding getting killed. 'There was only one catch and that was Catch–22,' wrote Heller, 'which specified that a concern for one's own safety in the face of dangers that were real and immediate was the process of a rational mind. Orr was crazy and could be grounded. All he had to do was ask; and as soon as he did, he would no longer be crazy and would have to fly more missions. Orr would be crazy to fly more missions and sane if he didn't, but if he was sane he had to fly them. If he flew them he was crazy and didn't have to; but if he didn't want to he was sane and had to. Yossarian was moved very deeply by the absolute simplicity of this clause of Catch–22 and let out a respectful whistle.' In a 'Catch–22' situation you are sure to lose whichever course of action you take.

Cavalcade

'Cavalcade' is the French word for a procession on horseback, which first appeared in English in the seventeenth century. Its origin lies in the Latin noun *caballus* meaning a 'pack horse'. When this passed into Italian, it changed into *cavalcata*. As cavalry techniques developed the simple procession was elevated to the status of a parade. With the disappearance of mounted cavalry from all but ceremonial occasions, the 'cavalcade' was taken up as a figurative expression for all kinds of elaborate public processions and parades.

Chink in your armour

A 'chink in your armour', either figurative or actual, is a weakness in your defences that leaves you vulnerable to attack. The analogy drawn by the modern meaning is that of the suits of armour worn by wealthy combatants, frequently knights and other gentry, in medieval conflicts. The purpose of armour was, self-evidently, to protect the wearer from injury. However, wear and battle damage could affect the intricate structure of a suit of armour, especially at its joints, thereby creating a small gap, or chink, through which a dagger or other narrow weapon could penetrate.

Chivalry

'Chivalry' was the knightly system of feudal times with its religious, moral and social codes and observances, which forms the backcloth to many tales of heroism and valour, notably those of King Arthur and his Knights of the Round Table. The English word is an anglicized form of the Old French noun *chevalerie*, which originated from the medieval Latin *caballerius*.

Clearing the decks

These days 'clearing the decks' frequently makes a cheerful reference to eating everything laid on a table at mealtimes. At a more serious level, the phrase carries the sense of removing everything that is not required for whatever action is about to be taken. In this it recalls its original usage at sea, when 'clearing the decks' of a warship formed part of the preparations immediately before going into action against an enemy.

Close quarters

The confined, frequently crowded, places referred to in the use of 'close quarters' today dates back to naval warfare of the eighteenth century, when it was common for opposing ships to run alongside each other enabling the crews to engage in hand-to-hand fighting. In these circumstances, the crew on a boarded ship, would retreat to pre-arranged points of defence, often behind protective barriers, from where they could fire on the enemy. Aboard ship these assigned positions were called 'close quarters' and, by extension, fighting from and around them became known as 'close quarters' combat.

Closing ranks

'Closing ranks' today means presenting a united front and this was its purpose on battlefields of the past, when armies lined up in ranks with the men standing shoulder to shoulder as they marched towards the enemy. Having no gaps between them, an approaching army presented a solid wall of armed attackers; an intimidating sight, especially when it was preceded by their similarly unbroken line of flashing swords or bayonets.

Coat of arms

Medieval knights wore surcoats of linen or silk over their armour to protetct it from the sun and dirt they encountered on their way to battle, notably on the way to fight in the Crusades. These coats were decorated with a knight's family crest, which was composed of symbolic elements representing details of the family history. When armour disappeared from warfare, the need for a protective coat went with it. However, its heraldic importance ensured its survival, usually in the form of a banner. Today a 'coat of arms' refers to the heraldic bearings of corporations and institutions as well as of individuals.

Cold enough to freeze the balls off a brass monkey

In spite of popular belief that places a decidedly crude meaning on this expression for extreme cold, its history reveals a perfectly respectable naval pedigree. Aboard eighteenth-century warships the word 'monkey' occurred in several terms connected with gunnery: boys who brought gunpowder to the guns were called 'powder monkeys'; there was a type of gun called a 'monkey'; and there was also a 'brass monkey' in the form of a plate attached to the deck, on which cannon balls were stacked ready for use. In very cold weather the brass contracted, unsettling the pile of cannon balls and causing them to fall down.

Colonel

A 'colonel' has always been the superior officer of a regiment, though in its earliest usage the word appeared in English as both 'colonel' and 'coronel'. These were related to similar words in French and Italian, notably the Italian *colonello*, the commanding officer of the first company of a regiment, a *colonna*.

Come to anchor

When a ship 'comes to anchor', the anchor is dropped into the water and the ship ends its voyage. Until the anchor is raised again at the start of the next voyage, the ship remains in harbour, firmly secured about its anchor-point. The same applies to an individual who 'comes to anchor'. In allusion to the ship ending its wanderings, a person who 'comes to anchor' settles down and stays in one place.

Commandeer

To 'commandeer' anything implies that it has been seized arbitrarily and often illegally. The term developed this meaning in English from the end of the nineteenth century, after it entered the language by way of British troops serving in the Boer War in South Africa, where they became familiar with the Boer use of the word, which meant 'to seize for military use'.

Conduct unbecoming

These are the two opening words of the phrase 'conduct unbecoming the character of an officer and a gentleman', which first appeared in the (British) Naval Discipline Act (10 August 1860), Article 24. As the phrase suggests, it detailed behaviour deemed to be unsuitable for an officer commissioned into the Royal Navy. Similar codes of conduct existed for the other services and for those in other countries. The playwright Barry England chose *Conduct Unbecoming* as the title for his 1969 play centred around army life in nineteenth-century British India.

Convoy

The origins of 'convoy' lie in the same roots as 'convey'. Both words carry a meaning of 'transport' and 'escort', which comes from the Old French verbs *conveier* and *convoyer*. Although 'convoy' was being used in English by the fourteenth century, it wasn't until the advent of submarine warfare in the twentieth century that the use of convoys became an established naval practice. During the First World War and more particularly during the Second World War, supply convoys of merchant ships from North America, protected by destroyers, maintained what Nicholas Monsarrat memorably described at the end of *The Cruel Sea*, his famous novel about the Battle of the Atlantic, as the 'golden prize – the uncut life-line to the sustaining outer world.'

Crossing the Rubicon

'Crossing the Rubicon' is an expression for taking an 'irrevocable step'; once crossed, there can be no turning back. The Rubicon referred to is a small river in northern Italy, which in Roman times marked the frontier between Italy and Cisalpine Gaul. The latter was the province under the control of Julius Caesar and when he crossed the Rubicon with an army in 49 B.C. he became an invader of Italy; an act which precipitated war with his rival Pompey and the Roman Senate.

Crusade

The original Crusades were a series of military campaigns undertaken by armies drawn from Christian countries in Europe, assembled to liberate the Holy Land from Islamic control. These spanned the eleventh to the fourteenth centuries and derived their present name from the French *croisade* and the Spanish *cruzada*, both of which are rooted in the respective words for 'cross' in those languages. The Christian cross was worn as a symbol on the shields and breastplates of the Crusaders and the zeal with which they fought has leant 'crusade' its present-day meaning; as both a noun and a verb it describes a forceful campaign in support of, or in opposition to, a particular action or issue.

Cut and run

The surest way of making a quick get away in a sailing ship was to cut the anchor rope and run before the wind. This meant losing the anchor, which would otherwise have had to be hauled aboard by hand; but that was a small price to pay if choosing to 'cut and run' saved the whole ship from capture by enemy vessels or destruction by fire-ships.

D-Day

Since the Second World War 'D-Day' has been used to describe an important day on which something was due to begin. During the war 'D-Day' was the code-name for the day on which the long-planned landings in northern France, marking the Allied invasion of Europe, were due to begin. In the detailed planning which led up to what became the Normandy landings, successive days became 'D-Day plus one' etc. Once the landings had taken place, the coded 'days' coincided with actual dates in the calendar; D-Day itself turned out to be 6 June 1944.

Deadline

These days a 'deadline' is a final time limit which must not be exceeded, but in its original context it was a physical line which was passed on pain of death. The term came into being during the American Civil War, when prisoners of war risked being shot on sight in many prison camps if they crossed a line marked some way inside the perimeter fence surrounding the camp. Understandably, this demarcation became known as the 'deadline'.

Decimating

In its modern usage 'decimating' means destroying on a large scale, or killing a very large proportion of a given number of people. However, the word originally had a far more specific meaning. In the Roman army at least one mutiny was punished by the execution of every tenth mutineer and the same punishment was sometimes inflicted on defeated armies. The Latin for 'ten' is *decem*, from which 'decimate' acquired its meaning as 'the killing of every tenth man', which persisted until the end of the nineteenth century.

Diehard

The original Die-Hards were members of the 57th Regiment of Foot who fought against Napoleonic forces in the Battle of Albuera, in Spain, on 16 May 1811. They were in the thick of the fighting and took heavy casualties. Out of a total of 570 who started the battle, the colonel, Sir John Inglis, twenty-two other officers and 400 men fell. Although mortally wounded, Inglis encouraged his troops in their advance, telling them not to surrender, but to 'Die hard'. Their bravery in the face of overwhelming odds helped secure a famous British victory. The regiment was nicknamed the Die-Hards and a 'diehard' has come to mean one who refuses to give in, no matter how hopeless his predicament.

COURAGE.

Digging in

Trench warfare, symbolized by the stalemate on the Western Front during the First World War, came to epitomize the military sense of 'digging in', when troops of both sides dug trenches, fortified them and used them during warfare, often without gaining or losing ground in any appreciable way. Since then anyone adopting an uncompromising position can be said to be 'digging in' and prepared for a lengthy stand-off before a resolution is reached.

Ditching

For RAF crews flying missions over occupied Europe during the Second World War, the English Channel became known as the 'ditch'. By association an aircraft that came down in the sea was said to have been 'ditched'. Ashore, the same bleak expression was applied to anyone left in the lurch. To be 'ditched' means, in terms of personal relations, to be left in the lurch and cast to one side.

Double-edged

'Double-edged' weapons date from ancient conflicts and, as the name suggests, were capable of inflicting harm when wielded in two different directions. The adjective has been applied in a figurative sense since the eighteenth century in phrases such as a 'double-edged compliment', meaning a comment that can have both favourable and unfavourable interpretations. So anything described as 'double-edged' is ambiguous and capable of simultaneously having opposite effects.

Double quick

In days gone by, the signal aboard warships calling hands to action stations was a rapid drumbeat which became known as the 'double'; hence expressions like 'on the double', 'at the double' and 'in double-quick time'.

Dragoon

A number of British cavalry regiments became known as 'dragoons' from the seventeenth century onwards. Use of the term derived from the name given to armed mounted infantry serving in the French army. These troops acquired it from the French noun for the weapon they carried, the carbine, known in French as a *dragon*, so called for its 'breathing fire' like a dragon. By extension, anyone unfortunate enough to have a detachment of dragoons set upon them could be described as being forced to comply with their demands; and this sense leant 'dragoon' its meaning as a verb, 'to coerce; and 'persecute'.

Drawing a bead on

To 'draw a bead' on an opponent literally means to take careful aim at them. The bead referred to is the foresight set on the barrel of a rifle or revolver. 'Drawing a bead' of this sort on anyone, implies getting them in your sights, ready for the kill.

Drawing a bow at a venture

Archery, and military archery in particular, has furnished English with a number of expressions that have long outlived the use of the longbow in warfare. 'Drawing a bow at a venture' is one of these turns of phrase, now meaning to attack without taking proper aim and, by analogy, to make a chance remark that coincidentally goes to the truth of a matter.

Draw the longbow

The prowess of the British archer with a longbow was well respected in medieval Europe. Celebrated victories like Crécy and Agincourt confirmed the fire-power and superiority of a well-trained corps of archers. In British folklore the skill of the archer was exemplified in the exploits of Robin Hood, so it was not unnatural for exaggerated claims to be made from time to time. While many archers could release arrows with such speed and power that they had six in the air at the same time, and some could shoot an arrow a mile, many could not. Boasting and false claims were easily disproved by a display of skill, or the lack of it. 'Drawing the longbow' proved the point then and figuratively makes the point now when someone is exaggerating.

Drill

In its modern usage 'drill' has two distinct meanings: as a tool for boring holes and as an exercise or practice, such as a fire 'drill', or the parade-ground exercises that form an important part of military and naval training. When 'drill' originated, however, the two meanings were closely linked. In German and Dutch the verb *drillen* was being used by the sixteenth century in the sense of 'boring' and 'turning in a circle'. At the same time soldiers were being instructed in movements which enabled them to turn about in an orderly way as a group. When *drillen* passed into English, it lost its last two letters and began to develop the meanings it has today.

Drummed out

Disgraced soldiers were ignominiously dismissed from military service by being formally expelled from their regiments to the accompaniment of beating drums. In civilian life, to be 'drummed out' implies a similar expulsion from an organization or institution.

Drumming up

In military camps and on the battlefield the drum was an important means of signalling orders to troops spread over a wide area. 'Drumming up' carries the meaning of calling together soldiers, or any other group, unexpectedly and often with a degree of urgency. Since its military origin it has spread into most walks of life: in the home, where a sudden influx of guests can result in a hastily 'drummed up' meal, and in the community, where the sudden need for volunteers or participants in a collective activity results in 'drumming up' support.

Dry run

Practice bombing flights were undertaken by RAF crews in the Second World War, who went through all the procedures of the forthcoming attack without dropping the bombs they would carry into action. Such practice missions became known as 'dry runs' and the term soon passed into general use to describe many forms of rehearsal and practice prior to an actual event.

Dubbing

Only a short time after the Norman Conquest of 1066, the word 'dub' entered the English language in the sense it still bears: investing with a dignity, specifically a knighthood. The Old French *adober* (only slightly modified in its present-day form *adouber*) meant to 'equip' with armour, which was part of the formal process of creating a knight, summed up by its English derivation. 'Dubbin' or ('dubbing'), the waterproof treatment applied to leather, also stems from the same source, extending the sense of a knight's equipment to its dressing and maintenance. The process of 'dubbing' which applies a soundtrack in one language to a film originally recorded in another has no connection with the sense of investiture; in this context 'dubbing' is an abbreviation of 'doubling'.

Dud

During the First World War artillery shells that failed to explode when fired from a gun became known as 'duds'. The expression then acquired a broader meaning to include anything that failed in its performance. However, prior to its twentieth-century usage, 'dud' was a term used to describe a weak or ineffectual person. The origin of this is unclear, but it may be associated with a name by which scarecrows were known from the seventeenth century. They were called 'dudmen' after their 'duds': the rags and tatters in which they were dressed.

Dum-dum

The soft-nosed bullet known in both military and civilian circles as a 'dum-dum' acquired its name at the end of nineteenth century from Dum Dum, a military station and arsenal near the Indian city of Calcutta.

Dutch courage

Whether justified, or not, the Dutch had a reputation during the seventeenth century as heavy drinkers. This was also the century in which Britain and the Netherlands were frequently engaged in wars at sea, from which the Dutch often emerged victorious. Among British sailors, it was widely believed that much of their success was due to being allowed to drink large quantities of gin before a battle. In these circumstances 'Dutch courage' was credited with winning the day and since that time a strong drink taken to brace oneself before an ordeal has also become known as 'Dutch courage'.

Dying in harness

In its military sense, 'dying in harness' meant falling in battle while dressed in armour and carrying weapons. 'Harness' in the context of body armour originated from a French word for military equipment in general, *harneis*, which itself may well have stemmed from an Old Norse word, *hernest*, meaning 'provisions for an army.' Thus Macbeth is able to throw himself into his final duel with Macduff at the end of Shakespeare's tragedy exclaiming,

> Ring the alarum bell! Blow, wind! come, wrack!
> At least we'll die with harness on our back.

Eating crow

'Eating crow' means to humiliate these days. The expression dates from an episode in the British-American War of 1812–14. During a ceasefire an American soldier out hunting inadvertently crossed the lines into territory held by the British army. Finding nothing more enticing to eat, he shot a crow. The sound of his musket alerted a British officer, who, though unarmed, was determined to teach the intruder a lesson. Pretending to admire the American's weapon, the officer succeeded in gaining hold of it, whereupon he turned it on the American and threatened to shoot him unless he ate a mouthful of the crow, which he reluctantly did. His point made, the British officer returned the musket to its owner, only to have the gun turned on him until he too had 'eaten crow'.

Echelon

'Echelon' is a direct English incorporation of the French noun *échelon* (a 'rung' of a ladder). The term was applied in the eighteenth and nineteenth centuries to a formation of troops lined up in parallel divisions but with no two on the same alignment. The overall appearance looked like a series of steps, or rungs on a ladder. Such military formations have disappeared from the battlefield, but 'echelons' remain in the language to describe groups with a particular authority or level of responsibility.

Egging on

If this expression was spelt 'edging on' its meaning would be more immediately apparent. 'Egging' in the sense of 'urging' and 'encouraging' is derived from the Old Norse for the sharp side of a blade, the *egg*. This is thought to be related to the Latin *acies*, meaning 'sharpness' as well as 'the edge of a blade'; *acus* a 'thorn' or 'needle' in Latin has a similar origin.

Enemy

Warfare would not be warfare without an 'enemy'. Enemies can be individuals, communities or whole nations, but they share the same characteristics of being hostile and unfriendly. The English 'enemy' comes directly from the Old French *enemi*. Words with a similar root are found in all Romance languages, stemming from the Latin *inimicus*, which carries the opposite meaning to the Latin for a friend, *amicus*.

Equerry

These days an 'equerry' is an officer of the royal household with specific duties to attend a member of the royal family. The modern spelling and pronunciation are associated with the Latin for a 'horse', *equus*. However, 'equerry' has closer connections with royal stables, than the horses kept in them. In its earliest forms 'equerry' appeared in Old French with various spellings, principally: *esquiry* and *escuirie*. The former is closely related to 'esquire' in English, the latter to the French for a stable, *écurie*. Brought together, the first 'equerries' were styled in French *escuyers d'escuyrie* ('squires of the stable').

Erk

Although anyone called an 'erk' these days might take offence, when the word was first coined it had favourable rather than pejorative connotations. 'Erk', or 'airk', dates from the early days of the RAF. A poem written in 1920, two years after the RAF came into being, made favourable references to service ground crew, who maintained aircraft and ensured they were fit for pilots to take into the air. The author of the poem, a pilot himself, wrote of aircraftmen,

> You fear no foe when up you go to keep the country free,
> Give me an airk who does not shirk; he's the boy for me.

Eyeball to eyeball

Commenting on the Cuban missile crisis of October 1962, when the Cold War was on the brink of becoming an all-out conflict, Dean Rusk (the US Secretary of State) made his well-remembered comment 'We're eyeball to eyeball, and I think the other fellow just blinked.' Confrontation cannot get much closer than 'eyeball to eyeball' and in using it, Secretary of State Rusk was following an idiom known among Black American servicemen. During the Korean War, staff at General MacArthur's headquarters enquired of the all-black 24th Infantry Regiment, 'Do you have contact with the enemy?' and received the answer, 'We is eyeball to eyeball.'

Facing the music

The military origin of this expression is similar to that of being 'drummed out', referring to the formal, humiliating dismissal of a soldier from his regiment. The ceremony involved the beating of drums, a public reading of the culprit's crime and the stripping of insignia from his uniform. Thus, 'facing the music' became associated with bearing punishment in general.

Fall out

To 'fall out' with someone is to quarrel or disagree with a person with whom you had formerly been close. As such it is a metaphor for the military command to 'fall out', by which troops standing close together in the ranks, were dismissed and allowed to disperse. Parting from a friend and going your separate ways is analogous to breaking what had previously been a close unity and bond.

Famous last words

This became a popular rejoinder among RAF bomber crews in the Second World War to official statements and assurances that minimized the risks they faced on forthcoming missions. It refers to the 'famous last words' uttered by the great on their death-beds, not a few of which proved to be ludicrously optimistic in the circumstances.

Feather in your cap

To have a 'feather in your cap' is to enjoy an honour or achievement of which you have a right to be proud. The expression recalls the heroic exploits of Edward the Black Prince, eldest son of Edward III of England, in the crushing victory over the French at the Battle of Crécy in 1346. After the battle, Prince Edward was awarded the crest of John, King of Bohemia, who had perished in the fighting. This showed the three ostrich feathers, which have been carried by every Prince of Wales since that time. The practice of wearing a feather in the helmet was subsequently taken up by any knight deemed to have fought well in later battles.

Fed up with

Commonly used as this phrase is as an expression for being 'bored with' or 'tired of' someone or something, it only became widely used during the twentieth century. Soldiers fighting in the Boer War right at the beginning of the century began describing South Africa, the campaigns and the conditions in which they lived in terms of being thoroughly 'fed up'. When they came home, they brought this term for 'being disgruntled' with them.

Field day

As an experience of great happiness and fulfilment, a 'field day' recalls a term dating from a couple of centuries ago, denoting a day in the army calendar set aside for manoeuvres and similar military exercises; an expression still in use today. By the mid-nineteenth century, civilians too were embarking on field days, though less arduous and significantly more enjoyable ones than those in which the troops were engaged.

Fifth column

A fifth column is a body of traitors, working secretly within a country or organization on behalf of an enemy or rival. Though widely used, the term is comparatively recent, dating from the Spanish Civil War of 1936–9. The Fascist army was divided into columns and General Mola, who commanded the Fascist forces advancing on Madrid, claimed that he had four columns surrounding the Spanish capital and a fifth working for him inside the city, undermining the efforts of the the defenders.

Fighting a losing battle

The connection with warfare at any stage in history is apparent in this phrase. To 'fight a losing battle' in combat is to maintain your resistance in the face of certain defeat. Transferred into a wider usage it carries the allusion of struggling on to the bitter end, knowing that defeat and failure is the inevitable outcome.

Fire away

Inviting someone to 'fire away' allows them to speak freely, giving voice to something that may well have been bottled up for some time. The analogy between this opportunity to speak out and the firing of a gun is obvious. 'Loaded' and 'primed for firing', the request to 'fire away' allows the speaker to 'discharge' what is on their mind.

First light

During the Second World War 'first light' became widely used to denote the earliest time of day at which there was sufficient light for military operations to begin or ships to go into action. Similarly 'last light' presented the latest time of the day at which such operations could be undertaken.

First rate

As an indication of the highest quality, 'first rate' originated in the Royal Navy, where all warships were once classified on a scale of one to six according to their size and the weight of armaments they carried. Leading ships were 'first rate' ones and from the navy the term passed into general use as a hallmark for excellence.

Flagship

In the Royal Navy a 'flagship' has traditionally been the vessel carrying a flag officer: an admiral, vice-admiral or rear admiral, who flies the flag of his rank. This distinction was adopted by merchant shipping companies who took to referring to the principal vessels in their fleets as 'flagships'. On land, the term 'flagship' is now applied to the foremost element or component of a wide range of enterprises and businesses.

Flak

German anti-aircraft artillery in the Second World War, known as *Fliegerabwehrkanone*, gave rise to the Allied acronym 'flak', which has now acquired the wider metaphorical meaning of 'severe adverse criticism'.

Flap

'Flap' is the commonly used slang for a panic, or situation of sudden, unexpected activity. It was popular among servicemen in the Second World War, probably as an extension of the nineteenth-century naval usage in which a 'flap' was slang among sailors for the order for a drill, or the command to change course to a number of warships; both of which entailed some commotion, especially when the orders resulted from the need to take emergency action. In this sense 'flap' is no doubt derived from the commotion caused by the beating of a bird's wings.

Flash in the pan

A 'flash in the pan' is an enterprise that begins brightly but soon fails after a very brief success. The allusion is to flintlock guns in which a small measure of gunpowder, ignited in the lockpan, detonated the main charge. It was not uncommon for the powder in the lockpan to fail to set off the charge in the breech. When this happened the 'flash in the pan' failed to carry out its objective.

Flat spin

'Flat spin' entered wider English usage from the terminology of flying. These days a 'flat spin' is an evasive manoeuvre in aerial combat, but in the early days of flying it was regarded as a spin in which the pilot lost control of the aircraft and it is in this sense that it has been generally adopted with the meaning of being 'very flurried' or 'in a panic'.

Flotilla

The small group of ships known as a 'flotilla' takes its name directly from the Spanish word of the same meaning, *flotilla*. This is the diminutive of *flota*, the Spanish for a 'fleet', from which that English word is similarly derived.

Fo'c'sle

When 'fo'c'sle' is spelt out in full as 'forecastle', its origin
becomes apparent. On medieval warships, the forward part of
the deck was raised as a castle-like structure designed to ride
above the deck of enemy ships, allowing troops inside it to fire
down on their adversaries. In time the 'fo'c'sle' became the part
of the ship in which the crew were quartered, leaving the rear
section of the ship (originally called the 'aftercastle') as
accommodation for the officers.

Forlorn hope

This expression meaning a 'vain hope', or an undertaking with
little chance of success, is an example of how a term in one
language can become mistranslated in another because of a
confusion of words with similar sounds. What in English
became 'forlorn hope' originated in Dutch as *verloren hoop* ('the

lost troop'), the term used for a body of troops, usually volunteers, who led the first wave of an attack, or who were the first into a breach made in a defensive fortification.

Freelance

Anyone who works 'freelance' today does so as an independent, self-employed worker. By analogy, a 'freelance' would appear to be a medieval warrior, not bound by feudal loyalty to a particular lord, but free to offer his services to whoever was prepared to pay him. This must have been the inspiration for Sir Walter Scott, for it was he who coined the expression 'freelance' in his medieval romance *Ivanhoe*, which dates from 1820. These days 'freelance' fighters are known as 'mercenaries'; in the Middle Ages they were called 'free companions'.

Furlough

Leave of absence from duty covered by the term 'furlough' was first recorded in English in the seventeenth century. It is a word borrowed from Continental usage. The Dutch *verlof* is the closest and this in turn is related to the German *verlaub*, which translated literally means 'for leave'.

Garret

By the fifteenth century 'garret' became the name for a small attic room of a house. Prior to this it had been used to describe a turret or watchtower, following the French word of the same meaning: *garite*.

Gen

The RAF was a fertile source for words and phrases which later became widely used in English. 'Gen', meaning 'important information' originated as a shortened form of 'general information' and soon became a verb, as in 'to gen up' on something, as well as a noun.

Get weaving

This is another vivid turn of phrase made popular during the Second World War and implying the need to set about a given task briskly. Added to this is the figurative image of the weaver, dexterously working between the warp and weft of a piece of cloth, just as an aircraft would take evasive action, rapidly altering course and altitude as it escaped enemy fire from ground and air.

Go ballistic

In modern warfare 'ballistic' missiles are largely unguided. Once launched and directed through the initial stage of its flight, a ballistic missile flies under its own power and falls freely towards its target. By analogy a person who 'goes ballistic' loses control and explodes in a violent, usually vociferous, rage.

Giving a wide berth

'Giving a wide berth' is the best course of action when someone has 'gone ballistic', or when you need to avoid getting involved with someone or something. The allusion is to the safe anchoring of ships, notably when a fleet was in port. Ships anchored at their 'berths' by the bow, which is the normal practice, swing about their anchorage points according to the direction of the wind and the movement of the tide. To avoid collision, it is important to ensure that adequate space is left between them; 'giving a wide berth' to another ship removes any chance of a mishap.

Going off at half-cock

Like a 'flash in the pan' this is another reference to the hazardous process of firing an old-fashioned flintlock gun, which involved releasing a spring-loaded hammer called a 'cock'. When released by the trigger, this struck a piece of flint against a steel plate, sending sparks into the small charge of powder in the lockpan, which in turn detonated the main charge in the breech of the gun. When the gun was fully cocked, it could only be discharged by pulling the trigger. 'At half-cock', however, it was liable to go off unexpectedly, often before there had been time to take aim, with the result that the shot was frequently wasted. That is why anything described as 'going off at half-cock' can be taken as premature, ill-prepared and unlikely to succeed.

Gone for a Burton

'Gone for a Burton' was another euphemism for 'missing, presumed dead' which became popular during the Second World War. No definitive explanation of its origin has been arrived at, but once again the RAF appears to have had a hand in its evolution. From the 1880s 'Burton-on-Trent' (often abbreviated to 'Burton') was rhyming slang for 'rent'. If the wartime connection lies here, it might allude to the missing serviceman paying his due, or possibly going missing to avoid paying rent. More likely is the brewing association with Burton-on-Trent which has been an important producer of beer for several hundred years. Aircrew shot down in the sea were said to have come down in 'the drink', thereby going for a beer or 'going for a Burton'. One other possible explanation links the expression with the British firm of men's tailors and outfitters called Burton. Above their headquarters in Blackpool, RAF signal operators were trained in Morse code and radio operation; those who failed their final assessment were said to have 'gone for a Burton'.

Gone west

In the First World War this became as popular a euphemism for dying in battle, as 'gone for a Burton' would be in the Second World War. The expression dates back to the sixteenth century and links death with the setting sun, which 'dies' in the west each evening.

Grapeshot

In the eighteenth century, artillery on both land and sea used 'grape-shot' as an effective ammunition against formations of closely packed troops. Unlike a cannon ball, which was a single projectile, grapeshot (as the name suggests) comprised small balls of cast iron shot, packed between iron plates and held together by a securing bolt. When fired, the grapeshot dispersed into a wide formation with devastating effects on the massed ranks against whom it was directed.

Graveyard shift

The midnight shift at factories or mills working twenty-four hours a day became known as the 'graveyard shift' during the First World War, because of the greater chance of accidents happening to workers employed at this 'unnatural' time of night.

Great guns

The shattering roar of a broadside fired from a late eighteenth-century warship no doubt gave rise to this naval expression for a violent gale, which was said to 'blow great guns'. Later it became a general term of emphasis, as in 'going great guns', which meant 'going flat-out, with full power and determination.'

Gremlins

A 'gremlin' is an unseen (and imaginary) imp or little devil that causes inexplicable mechanical malfunctions. Gremlins set to work in earnest during the Second World War, targeting the men and equipment of the RAF, who were the first of the services to point the finger of blame at them. The word 'gremlin' first appeared in print in 1929, but it was probably the serialization in 1942 of Roald Dahl's *The Gremlins*, that brought them to widespread public attention.

Grenade

The shape of a 'grenade' gives a clue to the origin of the word in several languages for this small, hand-thrown (and more recently rocket-propelled) missile. The first grenades entered military use in the sixteenth century and from the outset their shape and the way they exploded into fragments closely resembled the pomegranate fruit and the seeds that fill it, known in Old French as the *pumegrenate*. By the sixteenth century the small bomb had become a *grenade* in French and as such crossed the Channel to be adopted into English.

Grog

For over 200 years officers and men in the Royal Navy were issued with regular rations of watered down rum. These began in 1740 at the instigation of Admiral Vernon, who was then Commander-in-Chief West Indies. He was nicknamed Old Grog by the men under his command because of the cloak he habitually wore, which was made from grogram, a coarse material spun from silk and wool and stiffened with gum. It wasn't long before the admiral's nickname was applied to the daily rum ration and 'grog' gradually entered the language in a wider use, meaning all kinds of alcoholic drinks, including those which made the drinker feel 'groggy' as a result of over indulgence.

Grouse

British soldiers were using 'grouse' in the sense of 'grumble' by the end of the nineteenth century and through them the word entered general usage. How 'grouse' came into military slang is uncertain. In Old French *groucier* had the meaning of a 'grudge', but any relationship between this and the slang of a nineteenth-century British squaddie is almost certainly coincidental.

Guerilla

Just as *flotilla* was the diminutive of the Spanish noun *flota* (a 'fleet'), *guerilla* is the diminutive for *guerra*, which means 'war' in Spanish; and it was in Spain that the first so-called *guerilla*, or 'little war', was fought. Napoleon's invasion of Spain in 1808 provoked small bands of Spanish peasants to rise up against the invaders. British forces were sent to fight the French as well and in 1814 they, and their Spanish allies, won the Peninsular War. Thereafter any war fought by small bands of irregular troops using hit-and-run tactics has been known as a 'guerilla' war and the combatants fighting in it as 'guerillas'.

Gun

A heavy cannon was being referred to as a 'gun' in English as early as the fourteenth century, since when the word has grown to cover firearms of all sizes. 'Gun' is thought to be a shortened form of the Old Norse female name Gunnhildr, from *gunnr* (meaning 'war') and *hildr* (meaning 'battle'). The granting of female names to guns was not uncommon; in the fifteenth century a great gun called Mons Meg was installed in Edinburgh Castle.

Gung ho

In present-day use 'gung ho' is an adjective applied to an over-enthusiastic and often reckless approach to a task or situation. This represents a shift in meaning that has come about in just over half-a-century. When the expression was first coined in 1938, it meant 'work together', which was the English translation of the two Chinese characters representing this meaning and pronounced *kung ho*. The expression was used as the motto of the Chinese Industrial Co-operatives Association, which was established to provide employment for thousands of Chinese made refugees as a result of the Japanese invasion of their country. The phrase 'gung ho' found its way to the USA where it became the slogan for a battalion of Marines whose exploits in battle formed the basis for the 1943 film *Gung Ho!*

Gunwale

The 'gunwale' (or 'gunnel') is the upper edge of the side of a boat or ship, which formerly served to support the heavy guns aboard a warship. It originated as a combination of 'gun' and 'wale', the latter being the name for a ridge of various types, such as the one around a horse's collar, or a raised line in a fabric. A 'weal' raised on the flesh comes from the same sources: the Old Norse word *vala*, meaning a 'knuckle' and the old English word *walu*, 'a ridge of land'.

Half-mast

Flying a flag at 'half-mast', midway between the top and bottom of a flagpole, is a sign of mourning which originated in the navy as long ago as the seventeenth century as a mark of respect for the dead. In the last fifty years it has acquired the less respectful application that describes partly lowered trousers.

Hand over fist

These days 'hand over fist' is usually used to describe the easy and plentiful making of money, similar in meaning to 'coining it in' or 'pulling it in'. The last of these points to the naval origin of 'hand over fist', which developed aboard sailing ships when most of the work of hauling on ropes was done by hand. Whether pulling a rope to hoist a sail or for some other purpose, it moved between both hands and, in so doing, one hand passed over the fist of the other.

Hanging fire

In the days when guns were fired by igniting a fuse or a small charge of powder, those that were slow to discharge their projectiles were described as 'hanging fire'. The phrase was in common usage by the middle of the eighteenth century and by the beginning of the nineteenth was being used figuratively in the sense of hesitating or holding back.

Haversack

The first 'haversacks' were bags used to carry oats to feed cavalry horses; the name originated from the German words *haber* ('oats') and *sack* which is the same as its English equivalent. By the eighteenth century the 'haversack' had been incorporated into English with a change of meaning. Moving from a container for carrying provisions for horses, it had now become a smaller, general-purpose, shoulder bag for carrying a soldier's day rations. Since then 'haversacks' have been used to carry a variety of items, in both civilian and military life.

He has a famous bow up at the castle

This has a similar meaning to 'draw the longbow' and is used to chide those who boast about their exploits, or pretend to be something they manifestly are not.

Hectoring

Hector was the eldest and noblest son of King Priam of Troy. For ten years he led the Trojans in the defence of their city from the besieging Greeks until he was killed in battle by Achilles, who lashed Hector's body behind his chariot and dragged it in triumph three times around the walls. In life Hector was noble and magnanimous, which makes it all the more incongruous that his name should now be associated with 'hectoring', meaning 'bullying' and 'browbeating'. In Greek the adjective *hektor* means 'holding fast' and it is possible that this had given rise, by the seventeenth century, to an association in English with a 'swashbuckling', 'swaggering' fellow, 'holding fast' to his sword or, metaphorically, to his self-ordained status.

Hoist with his own petard

A 'petard' was a siege weapon made of iron and filled with gunpowder which was used in medieval warfare to blow a breach in a wall or fortified gate. Placing and detonating 'petards' was a hazardous process, not only from attack by defending troops, but also from the explosive device itself. Engineers who fired petards risked being killed by their premature explosion and one who perished in this way was 'hoist by his own petard'. The phrase has been used figuratively since then with reference to anyone who is caught in his own trap, or caught out by his own subterfuge.

Horde

In the thirteenth century the Mongol armies led by Genghis Khan conquered a huge tract of Asia which stretched from the Yellow Sea to the Black Sea. By the sixteenth century they and their Mongol successors were known in English as a 'horde', a term that has subsequently been applied to a very large number of animals or people, frequently on the move. 'Horde' is the English spelling of a word from the Turkic group of languages, *ordi*, meaning a 'camp'. Genghis Khan's grandson established a famous 'golden horde' at his camp in the area of Russia under his jurisdiction and the term gradually grew to encompass the whole Mongol military force, which amounted to virtually the entire nation.

Hors de combat

'Hors de combat' is a French expression that has moved directly into English. In French it means 'out of the battle' and originally referred to soldiers who were wounded or prevented from taking further part in the action. In its broader sense 'hors de combat' is used to mean 'out of the running' in any undertaking.

Infantry

'Infantry' comes from the same linguistic root as 'infant': the Latin adjective *infans*, meaning 'unable to speak'. 'Infant' was in use in English by the fourteenth century, with reference to a young child and two centuries later 'infantry' was a term being applied to foot soldiers, who were, for the most part, young and inexperienced in comparison with the knights who fought on horseback.

In the same boat

To be described as being 'in the same boat' as another person places you in the same predicament as them. The allusion here is to sailors who find themselves in a small boat at the mercy of the elements, knowing that whether they survive or perish, their destiny is the same.

Iron Curtain

This graphic metaphor for the hostile stand-off between the Soviet Union and its Communist allies and the non-Communist nations of Western Europe and North America following the end of the Second World War, was popularized by Sir Winston Churchill in a speech he gave at Fulton, Missouri, on 5 March 1946. However, he was not the first to use 'iron curtain' when referring to the Soviet Union or its sphere of influence. Ethel Snowden wrote of the 'iron curtain' she encountered in her 1920 book *Through Bolshevik Russia*; Josef Goebbels made use of it in *Das Reich* on 25 February 1945, and Sir Winston Churchill himself had included the phrase in a cable he sent to President Truman on 4 June 1945.

Jeep

The 'jeep' evolved in the Second World War as a general purpose, reconnaissance vehicle used by the US army. The initials 'GP' were printed on the sides of the first 'jeeps', which helped to spread the use of the acronym. However, the popularity and currency of the term was also due to 'Eugene the Jeep', a well-established character in the comic strip *Popeye the Sailor*. 'Eugene the Jeep' was an imaginary creature, free to move between different dimensions at will and able to make himself invisible. Given the versatility of his four-wheel-drive counterpart over all types of terrain, the wartime 'jeep' proved itself worthy of its name.

Jerrican

During the Second World War the German Afrika Korps carried spare fuel and water for its motor vehicles in square, box-shaped, containers. These were tough and versatile, easy to stack and easy to house on vehicles of all shapes. The British army soon adopted them for its own use and named the four-and-a-half-gallon cans 'jerricans' after their German (Jerry) inventors; 'Jerry' was a name used by British troops for a German, or Germans in general, since the First World War.

Kamikaze

'Kamikaze' is a Japanese word meaning 'divine wind', which refers to a providential typhoon that foiled a Mongol invasion of Japan in the thirteenth century. In the last year of the Second World War it was applied to suicide bombing missions undertaken by Japanese pilots. Between October 1944 and the beginning of 1945 an estimated 5,000 Japanese pilots were killed when they deliberately crashed their bomb-laden planes into targets. Today 'kamikaze' is applied to a rashly foolhardy rather than an intentionally suicidal actions.

Kaput

This word meaning 'broken', 'finished' or 'dead' is the English version of the German *kaputt*, which means 'done for' and 'ruined'.

Keel-hauling

Luckily for those subjected to a 'keel-hauling' today, they usually escape with a severe reprimand. This is a far cry from the original 'keel-hauling': a form of brutal punishment that was once current in the Royal Navy. Those unfortunate, or guilty, enough to be sentenced to a keel-hauling, were bound and literally hauled underneath the ship from one side to the other, receiving terrible lacerations and often drowning in the process.

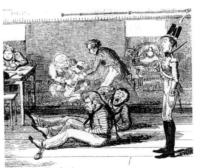

Khaki

'Khaki' is a colour most closely associated with military uniforms. A dull brownish-yellow, it was first used to dye the fabric of British army uniforms during the Indian mutiny of

1857. Indeed, 'khaki' is the Urdu word for 'dusty', which derives from *khak*, the Persian word for 'dust'.

Kissing the gunner's daughter

This was a grim euphemism for a flogging in the Royal Navy, because at one time sailors sentenced to a flogging were tied to the breech of a gun.

Last-ditch

In the military tactics of days gone by the 'last ditch' was the last line of defence. Therefore, a 'last-ditch' attempt is a final desperate effort; the one resorted to when every other avenue has been tried. The same sense of holding on to the very end is conveyed by the expression 'to die in the last ditch', a phrase that was used by King William III who, in answer to a question from the Duke of Buckingham, 'Do you not see your country is lost?', replied 'There is one way never to see it lost and that is to die in the last ditch.'

Legion

A large number of people these days is sometimes referred to as a 'legion' because the original 'legions' were very sizeable gatherings of soldiers varying in number from 4,200 to 6,000 men in each one. These were the legions of the Roman army, huge bodies of troops divided into ten cohorts per 'legion'. The Latin for a 'legion' is *legio*, which is derived from *legere*, a verb meaning 'to gather', 'to collect' and 'to pick'.

Living quarters

The origin of 'quarter' in the sense of 'living quarters' is the French verb *écarter*, meaning 'to separate' or 'to set apart'. In this context 'living quarters' are those parts of a military base designated for accommodation; so 'married quarters' are those for married personnel and 'officers' quarters' ones set aside as accommodation for officers.

Logistics

Accommodation had a part to play in the origin of 'logistics', a word now widely used in the sense of organizing equipment, materials and people to ensure that everyone and everything needed for a particular undertaking is in the right place, at the right time. Originally 'logistics' was confined to military and naval use. It stemmed from a nineteenth-century French term *logistique*, which carried the same meaning. This, in turn, was derived from the French *loger* ('to quarter'), from which the English 'lodge' also comes. One of the key tasks of the French 'logistics' officer was to find accommodation for his troops.

Long shot

These days a 'long shot' is a synonym for a 'wild guess', but in the warfare of earlier times, before the introduction of pinpoint accuracy with guided missiles, a 'long shot' was one fired at so great a distance from a target, that the chance of hitting it was very slim.

Loophole

Defenders of medieval castles made use of 'loopholes' to spy on their enemies and shoot at them. For reasons of security and personal safety, loopholes were necessarily small, narrow gaps in the castle walls. Referred to simply as 'loops' in the fourteenth century, these gaps had become 'loopholes' by the sixteenth. In later centuries 'loopholes' changed in meaning to be less a means of defending somewhere than a narrow, easily overlooked, way of escape. This is the meaning that has come down to us today, when a 'loophole' has become 'a way out of' an obligation or legal requirement; frequently a 'gap' inadvertently left in a piece of legislation that is then exploited by the sharp-eyed and quick-witted. In this sense 'loophole' may owe something to the Dutch word *loopgat*, formed from *loop* ('to run') and *gat* ('a way').

Loose cannon

The image conveyed by 'loose cannon' envisages the damage and mayhem that could be caused aboard a warship if one of its heavy artillery pieces broke loose from its mounting and rolled free over a gundeck during a storm or in the course of a battle. The phrase came into common usage early in the nineteenth century and since then has been applied metaphorically to people who are inclined to behave uncontrollably and without due regard to the consequences of what they say or do.

Mace

These days a 'mace' is a purely ceremonial staff of high office, pertaining to the sovereign and high officers such as the Speaker of the House of Commons and the mayors of certain cities and towns. Originally, a 'mace' was a fearsome weapon: a club with a metal head and wielded in battle with devastating effect. As such it was derived from the Latin *mattea* ('a club') and passed into English by way of the Old French *masse*. Modern French retains this meaning of *masse*, which translates into English as a 'sledgehammer'.

Magazine

The modern 'magazines' lining the shelves of newsagents are periodicals containing articles written by various authors, the first of which to be published was *The Gentleman's Magazine* that appeared in 1731. This contained in its *Introduction* an explanation of how the use of 'magazine' was arrived at in a literary context: 'This consideration has induced several Gentlemen to promote a Monthly Collection to treasure up, as in a Magazine, the most remarkable Pieces on the Subjects above mention'd'. Prior to that, 'magazine' had been applied to 'a storehouse of information' and both uses draw on the original meaning of the word derived from the Arabic *makhazin* which was also a 'storehouse'; latterly one specifically for arms and munitions, a meaning that is still in use in English today.

Mailed fist

This is an expression of aggressive military force, made famous by William II of Germany, who urged Prince Henry of Prussia to use the *gepanzerte Faust* during the tour of the Far East on which he was about to depart in December 1897. 'Should anyone essay to detract from our just rights or to injure us,' his brother told him, 'then up and at him with your mailed fist'. The analogy is to the glove made from 'mail', which was worn by medieval knights as part of their battle armour. 'Mail', in the sense of rings or plates of armour, was derived from the French *maille* ('mesh'), which has its roots in the Latin *macula*, meaning 'a spot', referring to the holes between the links in the mesh.

Magenta

The bright crimson colour known as 'magenta' acquired its name from the town of Magenta, slightly to the west of Milan in northern Italy, where an exceptionally bloody battle was fought in 1859 between the Austrians and a combined army of French and Sardinian troops. Only a short time after the battle, a brilliant red aniline dye was discovered and named Magenta to commemorate the battle which had resulted in such appalling carnage.

Make and mend

A period designated as 'make and mend' is one without any specific task allotted to it. The expression originated in the

Royal Navy when particular afternoons were set aside as 'make and mend' periods in which the crew could make and repair their clothing and personal equipment.

Marathon

Few events in ancient history are widely remembered or recalled today, but the Battle of Marathon fought in 490 B.C. has been firmly planted in languages around the world thanks to the long-distance running races named after it. Marathon was a decisive battle fought between the Athenians and Persians, from which the Athenian army emerged victorious. News of the triumph was carried to Athens by a runner who covered the twenty-three miles, delivered his message and then died from his exertions. When the modern Olympic Games were instituted in 1896 the Marathon became one of its events. In 1924 the distance of the race was standardized at 26 miles 385 yards (42.052 kilometres). Marathon races have subsequently become popular at other athletic competitions and as events in their own right in which thousands of competitors take part. 'Marathon' has also become established as an adjective for any feat requiring great endurance.

Marching orders

As well as referring to commands given to troops to move on, giving 'marching orders' is now a euphemism for dismissing someone from a job. This general meaning came into use during the eighteenth century.

Marking time

In whatever sense it occurs, 'marking time' means that nothing happens. Used figuratively it amounts to a holding operation, keeping things going while waiting for something to happen. In its military sense, 'marking time' is a parade-ground drill in which troops raise their feet in a marching rhythm without moving forwards or backwards.

Moaning Minnie

'Moaning Minnie' was the slang name given by Allied troops in the First World War to a type of German trench mortar, called a *Minenwerfer*, or the shell fired from it which made a distinctive moaning noise in flight. During the Second World War, 'Moaning Minnie' was also applied to air-raid sirens, which made a similar 'moaning' sound. From these wartime uses, the expression has become more widely applied to a habitual moaner and grumbler.

Molotov cocktail

Soviet Foreign Minister Vyacheslav Molotov is best remembered these days for the linking of his name with the type of home-made, hand-thrown, inflammable bomb known as a 'Molotov cocktail'. In its earliest form it was a simple, but effective, device comprising a bottle filled with petrol or some other inflammable liquid, fitted with a slow-burning fuse (often a piece of rag). Bombs of this type were used during the Spanish Civil War, but their particular association with Molotov followed the Russian invasion of Finland in the 'Winter War' of 1939. Finnish fighters, who used 'Molotov cocktails' to some effect against Russian tanks, regarded Molotov as the personification of Russian aggression.

Mufti

In the nineteenth century, officers, who were off-duty in their quarters, often dressed in flowered dressing-gowns, slippers and tasselled smoking-caps which bore a strong resemblance to the stage costume of characters representing Eastern holy men, known in Arabic as *muftis*. It seems likely that the wider use of 'mufti', to describe clothes worn off-duty by those who on-duty would be in uniform, originated from what was seen at that time as a humorous association of appearances.

Musket

The musket was an early handgun used in battle by the infantry. As such its name harks back to a weapon it replaced: the crossbow which fired a bolt, known in Italian as a *moschetto*. This derived its name from *musca*, the Latin for 'a fly'.

Nailing your colours to the mast

Military or naval flags ('colours') are hoisted to the top of a flagpole and secured in place by lines. However, these are vulnerable to being shot away in battle, which could be demoralizing especially as lowering your colours was a signal of surrender. To avoid this risk, 'colours' could be nailed to the mast, an act which also ensured that they could not be lowered in submission and defeat. Therefore, 'nailing your colours to the mast' shows the intention of refusing to give in.

Napoo

Despite the debt English owes to French for supplying much military terminology, English soldiers seldom made much headway with the language when they were fighting in France. 'Napoo' is one example of their attempts to make the best they could of French. It was coined in the First World War and meant 'nothing'; that being the closest the British squaddie could get to *il n'y en a plus* ('there's nothing left').

Nazi

This is the abbreviated form of *National-Sozialist*, the name given to Adolf Hitler's political party, which is still current in expressions like 'neo-Nazi', referring to extreme right-wing, racist groups, who pursue their political and social aims with the same thuggish brutality as Hitler's supporters.

Near miss

During the Second World War ships under attack from enemy aircraft recorded a 'near miss' for every bomb that exploded in the water close enough to cause some damage to the hull. Since then its meaning has broadened to include any mishap that has been narrowly avoided.

Nelson touch

Any action recalling the tactics or leadership of Horatio Nelson has been known as the 'Nelson touch' since Nelson himself used the phrase, only three weeks before his death at the Battle of Trafalgar on 21 October 1805. Writing to Lady Hamilton on 1 October, he told her, 'I believe my arrival was most welcome, not only to the Commander of the Fleet but almost to every individual in it; and when I came to explain to them the "*Nelson touch*", it was like an electric shock.'

Nom de guerre

A French expression meaning 'war name', *nom de guerre* is generally used in the sense of an 'assumed name'. Its origin lies in the time-honoured practice of entrants into the French army assuming names. This was particularly prevalent in the Middle Ages when knights were known by the devices painted on their shields.

No names, no pack-drill

This phrase, conveying refusal to identify people in order to prevent the possible apportionment of blame, recalls an obsolete army punishment known as 'pack-drill', which involved marching up and down in full marching order. Figuratively the expression means that it is impossible to slander or libel someone whose name is unknown.

No quarter given

This stark phrase carries the grim consequence of defeat in days gone by, when it was not uncommon for prisoners to be killed. To give 'no quarter' equates to granting no mercy to a captive and may originate from the need to provide prisoners with accommodation, or 'quarters'. With 'no quarter given' the need to find shelter for a defeated enemy was removed, thereby allowing the victors to take for themselves whatever shelter (and sustenance) was available.

Nothing to write home about

As the phrase suggests, 'nothing to write home about' expresses the view that there is nothing remarkable or worthy of comment about a particular place, individual, or set of circumstances. It was an expression already known in English before the First World War, but it was the stationing of many thousands of British troops in France that brought it to the fore.

Old Contemptibles

The British Expeditionary Force sent to France in 1914 at the outbreak of the First World War, was apparently described by the German Kaiser as 'a contemptible little army'. Other accounts report him as saying 'a contemptibly little army'. Whichever it was, members of that first British force in France became known as the Old Contemptibles.

Old Guard

The stalwarts of any party or movement are known as the 'Old Guard' after the veteran regiments of Napoleon's Imperial Guard. The cream of the French army, the Old Guard could be relied on to hold steady in the most desperate action and it was the Old Guard that made the last French charge at the Battle of Waterloo.

On the stocks

'The stocks' in this expression is the frame on which a ship is placed during its construction. All the time that work continues on it the ship is said to be 'on the stocks', so giving rise to the wider meaning of the phrase: for something to be in hand but not yet completed.

Oppo

In the Royal Navy and the RAF an 'oppo' was an abbreviation for an 'opposite number', in other words a pal, or mate. The word was also applied, with slightly stronger affection one assumes, to wives and sweethearts.

Outgunning

In its metaphorical use 'outgunning' carries a sense of 'overwhelming' or 'outdoing' by virtue of superior 'force' of whatever form. The term, self-evidently, comes from the deployment of superior battlefield artillery, which produced greater firepower than that of the enemy; it dates from the late seventeenth century.

Over the top

Abbreviated these days to the initials 'OTT', 'over the top' now carries the somewhat pejorative sense of exaggeration and excessively showy display. The original meaning dates from the First World War, when the first part of any attack on the Western Front involved going 'over the top'. This entailed both climbing out over the top of the front-line trench in which the troops had gathered and advancing through No-man's Land (also referred to as 'the top').

Parthian shot

In the ancient world Parthian warriors, who at one time held sway over a large area of Asia stretching from present-day Iraq to Pakistan, were renowned for their skill as mounted archers. While riding away from an enemy, in either a real or feigned retreat, they could turn back in the saddle and fire arrows at their pursuers. So a Parthian shot became, by analogy, a 'parting shot', a final remark passed in such a way that your opponent has no chance of responding.

Parting brass-rags

In the Royal Navy it was common for ratings to share everyday cleaning equipment with a colleague, such as the rags used to clean a ship's brass. When two friends quarrelled such sharing came to an end and they were said to be 'parting brass rags'.

Passing muster

'Passing muster' amounts to measuring up to a required standard and originates from a military parade ('muster') at which troops were assembled to be inspected. 'Muster' entered English from the Old French *moustre*, which was itself derived from the Latin verb *monstrare* ('to point out' and 'to show').

Phalanx

The original 'phalanx' was a fighting formation of armed men deployed by Greek armies in the ancient world. The use of tightly-packed spearmen in the phalanx was developed by the Spartans but reached its peak of military efficiency and prowess in the Macedonian armies commanded by Philip of Macedon and his son Alexander the Great. The same sense of close unity that is found in any group of people banded together with a common purpose remains in the present-day use of 'phalanx'.

Picket

In French a *piquet* is a 'pointed stake' which served several purposes on the battlefield. They acted as tent pegs; they could also be used to 'picket' (tether) horses; and, turned point-up, they formed an outer defence works. From this latter meaning 'picket' also began to be applied to small detachments of troops sent out beyond the defensive ring to watch for the advancing enemy. In the middle of the nineteenth century 'picket' started to apply to small groups of workers placed at the entrance to work places, to look out for those going to work during a strike.

Pile

Heavy posts made of concrete or steel that are driven into soft ground to form support for a structure are known as 'piles' and a group of them driven in together is known as 'piling'. The English word is similar to ones of the same meaning in other northern European languages and all originate in the Latin *pilum* meaning a 'javelin', which was the Roman infantry soldier's principal weapon.

Pile-up

This popular euphemism for an accident involving mechanized transport originated in the Royal Navy where a 'pile-up' involved running a ship aground. In the RAF 'piling up your bus' meant crashing your aircraft. And in civilian life a 'pile-up' has become an accident involving motor vehicles that are buckled and bent into heaps by the force of their impact.

Pillbox

The use of small, shallow cylindrical boxes to hold pills dates from the middle of the eighteenth century. By the end of the nineteenth the term 'pillbox' had passed into military use to describe the type of cap worn by soldiers in several national armies; the same shape of hat later became fashionable in women's *haute couture*. During the First and Second World Wars, the term pillbox was applied to small, low, reinforced concrete bunkers, often partially buried in the ground and used as machine-gun posts.

Pinning to your sleeve

In the medieval world where chivalry and courtly love held sway, knights were in the habit of pinning to their sleeves tokens given to them by their lady-loves. In doing this they pledged to succeed in whatever endeavour they were undertaking or to die in the process. The same sense of unremitting commitment is carried into the present-day use of the phrase, in expressions like 'I'm pinning my hopes to your sleeve.'

Pitched battle

A 'pitched battle' is a planned battle, that takes place on a predetermined site. In this sense 'pitch' has been used in English since the thirteenth century.

Plonk

We have British troops fighting in France during the First World War to thank for the word which is now generally used to describe most cheap wine. Encountering French white wine, the British soldier soon substituted the word 'plonk' for *vin blanc* ('white wine') and English speakers throughout the Commonwealth have been knocking back plonk from wine-producing countries all over the world ever since.

Point-blank

'Point-blank' originated as an artillery term from which it has developed the broader meaning of 'direct' and 'straight to the mark'. In early gunnery, a cannon aligned in such a way that it fired directly at a target, hitting it in a straight line, without any curve in the projectiles' flight, was said to be fired 'point blank'. In order to achieve this, the targets had to be comparatively close and here the expression recalls its earlier derivation on the field of archery practice. In French the *point blanc* ('white mark') is the bull's eye of a target. In order to be sure of hitting this, an archer needed to fire from a fairly close range, sighting the line of his arrow straight at the the centre of the target.

Point of no return

A 'point of no return', both figurative and actual, is a position or situation from which there is no turning back. During the Second World War the phrase became current amongst aircrew who knew that once they had reached the 'point of no return' there was not enough fuel to return to base, leaving no choice but to continue to another destination.

Poppy day

As another name for Remembrance Day, 'Poppy Day' entered the language following the First World War and the appearance of artificial poppies made and sold by the Royal British Legion to raise funds for the support of veterans of all military conflicts and actions. The poppy, which grows abundantly in European corn fields, appeared in profusion in the battlefields of northern France during the First World War, its bright red colour providing a vivid symbol of the terrible bloodshed on the Western Front. On 3 May 1915, Dr John McCrae, who was serving with the Canadian Army Medical Corps in Ypres, wrote a poem entitled 'In Flanders Fields', which opens with the memorable lines,

> In Flanders fields the poppies blow
> Between the crosses, row on row,
> That mark our place.

This was published in *Punch* at the end of 1915 and struck a chord with the British public which adopted the poppy as a symbol of the loss and suffering in that and all subsequent wars. Dr McCrae was killed in 1918, the year in which the First World War ended.

Prang

'Prang' was popularized by use in the RAF, where it had two meanings. In one sense 'prang' was employed to describe the crash-landing of an aircraft and this is the use to which it is put today when referring to a road collision that is usually less serious than a 'pile-up'. The other wartime meaning of 'prang' was a heavy attack from the air and here there may be connections with the Malay words *perang*, meaning 'war' and *perangi*, 'to attack'.

Pummel

To 'pummel' someone is to pound them with your fists, although the original meaning was to beat with them with the 'pommel' of your sword, rather than strike them with the blade. On a sword the 'pommel' is the rounded knob at the bottom of the hilt, named, because of its rounded shape, after the French for an apple (*pomme*).

Pyrrhic victory

In 279 B.C. Pyrrhus, King of Epirus, led a sizeable army against the Romans at the Battle of Asculum. Although his forces won, the cost in casualties was so great that Pyrrhus has been remembered for his comment 'One more such victory and we are lost.' Since that time the term 'Pyrrhic victory' is given to all successes that are so costly they amount to defeats.

Quarterdeck

This is another borrowing from the French *écarter*, meaning 'to set apart'. Here it refers to the rear section of a ship that was set aside for officers, whereas the main body of the crew were 'quartered' in the fo'c'sle, situated towards the bows. The 'quarterdeck' itself was the raised part of the deck running aft from the mainmast to the stern; in the Royal Navy it was traditionally the promenade reserved for officers.

Raglan sleeve

A 'raglan' sleeve is a style of sleeve without shoulder seams, the sleeves extending up to the neck. It takes its name from a style of coat popularized by Lord Raglan, the British commander in the Crimean War. An overcoat without shoulder seams acquired his name and in due course so did its style of sleeves.

Rally

As a verb, 'rally' means 'to enlist support' or 'to lend support'. As a noun, a 'rally' is a gathering brought together to generate interest in and enthusiasm for a cause. Both senses are drawn from the French *rallier*, which means 'to assemble troops' and has the figurative application of 'to win votes or support'. On the battlefield, rallying the troops served to bring together forces that had become scattered; in so doing they were literally 're-allied' and *rallier* comes from the same root as *allier*, from which 'ally' is derived.

Rank and file

In military terms 'rank' refers to troops in line abreast, 'file' to soldiers standing one behind the other. Together, 'rank and file' came to be used as a general term to distinguish ordinary soldiers and non-commissioned officers from commissioned officers. In the same way, the 'rank and file' of any group or movement are the members as distinct from the organizers and leaders.

Rearguard action

'Rearguard' is derived from the old French *rereguarde*, (later *arrière-guarde*), and refers to the back section of an armed force. It was used in this sense in English by the fifteenth century. As military strategy developed, the 'rearguard' became detached from the main force, in order to protect it from attack from behind. A defensive measure of this sort became known as a 'rearguard action' and away from battlefield usage it is also employed in reference to any attempt to support or defend a cause or campaign which is effectively 'in retreat' or in decline.

Rebel

The Latin for 'war' (*bellum*) is the source for 'rebel', which came into being in English by way of the French *rebelle*. Both of these recall another Latin word *rebellis*, which was applied to an uprising by people who had previously been conquered; in other words who made war afresh. From this has stemmed the current meaning of 'rebel' which, as both noun and verb, is applied to people and actions that disregard obedience or allegiance.

Recce

'Recce' is the abbreviated and more modern version of 'reconnaissance'. This is a direct borrowing from French in which the same word carries the same meaning of ascertaining the location and strength of an enemy force. 'Reconnaissance' originates from the verb *reconnaître* ('to recognize'), which derived from the Latin verb of the same meaning *recognoscere*.

Red Cross

The terrible suffering of men wounded in the Battle of Solferino in 1859 led to the calling of an international conference in the Swiss city of Geneva in 1864. This resulted in the Geneva Convention, which provided guidelines for the care of the wounded and captured in wartime. In addition, military medical services were to be protected under the internationally recognized symbol of a 'red cross' (sometimes called the Geneva Cross). A red cross on a white background, this was a reversal of the Swiss national flag: a white cross on a red background.

Rendezvous

As a 'prearranged meeting', 'rendezvous' is derived from the French *rendez-vous*, a command originally given to troops meaning 'present yourselves', which in due course was applied to a place where troops assembled. 'Rendezvous' has been used as a verb in English since the seventeenth century and has gradually acquired its broader meaning in both English and French.

Riding roughshod over

Those in the habit of 'riding roughshod over' others act with complete disregard for their feelings or interests. The expression originated among battlefield cavalry units of days gone by, in which horses were sometimes fitted with special shoes with sharp projections and cutting edges. These were intended to add further terror to the foot-soldiers against whom they went into action and who would suffer terribly from being ridden over by 'roughshod' cavalry.

Right-hand man

As a valued helper, a 'right-hand man' is a key assistant to the leader of any organization; metaphorically, he is as important as the leader's own right hand. The term also has a military origin, referring to the man stationed at the extreme right of a line of infantry or cavalry. This was an important position that carried special responsibilities in executing manoeuvres and keeping the line straight and which sometimes entailed a degree of command.

Run amok

Troops, or anyone else, who 'runs amok', are seized with a sudden, uncontrollable frenzy, which often results in violence and damage. The word 'amok' (or 'amuck') comes directly from the Malay language in which *amog* is a 'state of frenzy'.

Run the gauntlet

To 'run the gauntlet' is to be criticized and attacked on all sides. The expression appeared in English during the Thirty Years War in the first half of the seventeenth century. When it was first used 'gauntlet' was spelt *gantlope*, this being a Swedish word formed from *gata* ('a lane') and *lopp* ('a course'). It referred to a punishment current in the Swedish armed forces in which those sentenced were made to pass between the crew or company drawn up in two lines forming a narrow gap between them. Armed with rope ends, or other appropriate weapons, every man in the line beat the miscreant, while he 'ran the gauntlet'.

Sabotage

'Sabotage' is a comparatively recent arrival in both French and English. Without doubt acts of 'sabotage' took place centuries before the word was coined, but it came into general use following a strike by French railway workers in the nineteenth century. As part of the disruptive action to further their cause, they loosened or removed the shoes that secured the iron rails to their wooden sleepers; so making it impossible to run trains along those sections of track. In French such shoes are called *sabots*, the same word that is given to the wooden clogs worn by French peasants. The verb *saboter* carries an additional meaning of 'doing something poorly.'

Sacrament

In Christian worship a 'sacrament' is a religious ceremony or act symbolizing or conferring grace, of which the two most widely recognized are baptism and the Eucharist. In the Latin New Testament, *sacramentum* is given the meaning of 'sacred mystery', but the word had an earlier military usage in pre-Christian Rome, where it referred to the solemn oath taken by every Roman soldier not to abandon the colours, or his commander, and not turn his back on the enemy.

Sailing under false colours

At sea, ships were historically identified by their colours, the flags they flew showing to which nation, or company, they belonged. It was common for pirates to fly 'false colours' in order to approach unsuspecting victims close enough to launch successful attacks. In times of war 'sailing under false colours' was regarded as an underhand way of deceiving an enemy at sea and led to the adoption of the phrase in a wider context when reference was needed to acting hypocritically, or seeking to achieve your end by false pretences.

Salient

On a battlefield, particularly one in which troops are dug in, a 'salient' is a section of the front line that juts out from the rest. The same word applies to medieval fortifications in which 'salients' were created to provide projections in the defences that allowed defenders a wider range from which to see and fire at their attackers. In both cases 'salient' is derived from the Latin *salire* meaning 'to leap'.

Sam Browne belt

The 'Sam Browne' is a distinctive style of leather belt which first became part of a British army officer's and warrant officer's uniform during the second half of the nineteenth century and was soon adopted by military and police forces in many parts of the world. The belt was invented by General Sir Sam Browne, a distinguished veteran of the Indian Mutiny of 1857, and comprised a broad belt around the waist with a thinner one over the shoulder; this was intended to support the weight of the wearer's sword and prevent it from causing the main belt to sag.

Scout

A 'scout' today performs the same basic task as his medieval counterpart: obtaining information. Today 'scouts' operate in a a variety of contexts: sports teams, for instance, employ scouts to seek out potential players. When the word was first used in English it had a specific military sense, based on the Old French verb *éscouter*, meaning 'to listen' (the modern word is *écouter*). Those who were sent out ahead of an army to spy on an enemy were effectively 'listeners'. In time the meaning of the word was extended to cover all forms of reconnoitring.

Send to Coventry

The origin of this well-known phrase seems to derive from the particular dislike the people of Coventry had at one time for soldiers. During the English Civil War, Royalist soldiers captured in Warwickshire were sent to the Parliamentary stronghold of Coventry, where the citizens made it plain what they thought of them and their cause. It was also said that any woman in Coventry seen talking to a soldier was immediately ostracized by her townsfolk. No doubt attitudes in Coventry have changed radically since those times, but the expression is still used as a term for humiliating a person by completely ignoring him or her.

Serving before the mast

This expression comes from the days of sailing ships and refers to ordinary seamen who were quartered in the fo'c'sle: the part of a ship which lay forward of the main mast, in other words 'before the mast'.

Seven bells

To knock 'seven bells' out of someone or something implies giving a severe beating. The phrase originated in the Royal Navy, though why seven should have been the chosen number remains unresolved.

Shooting your bolt

In medieval archery a 'bolt' was the short, blunt arrow fired from a crossbow. Although powerful and accurate, crossbows were cumbersome weapons to reload and as a result had a far slower rate of fire than the longbow. With only one bolt to shoot at a time, an archer who had shot his bolt had nothing with which to attack (or possibly defend himself) until he reloaded the next. From this we get the present-day meaning of 'shooting your bolt', to have tried your utmost, expending all your resources.

Show a leg

This traditional naval command to get up in the morning dates from the time when women were allowed in the crew's quarters aboard ship. When the sailors were called out in the morning, the waking call was 'Show a leg or a purser's stocking', and any leg that appeared in a stocking indicated that there was a woman in the hammock, who would be allowed to remain until the men had gone on deck. From the time when women were no longer tolerated below decks, the reference to the stocking was dropped and the phrase shortened to become a general 'wake-up' call.

Show a white feather

'A white feather' is a symbol of cowardice which originated in the days of cock fighting, when 'to show the white feather' was a euphemism for cowardice, since no pure-bred gamecock had any white feathers in its plumage. Any bird found with even a single white feather was evidently from inferior stock and could not be expected to show the fighting characteristics of a thoroughbred. During the First World War the habit developed among a section of deeply 'patriotic' women of handing white feathers to men of fighting age they came across wearing civilian clothes; the implication being that if they were not in uniform they had to be cowards.

Showing the white flag

By universal acknowledgement an all-white flag is a symbol of surrender, or at the very least a desire to cease fighting and discuss a truce. By the same understanding, anyone carrying a white flag is immune from harm.

Shrapnel

In 1806 a British general named Henry Shrapnel serving in the Peninsular War devised a type of artillery shell comprising small metal balls and an explosive charge detonated by a time fuse. This was designed to be fired from a cannon, exploding before it reached its target and thereby scattering a shower of small projectiles among the enemy. The original Shrapnel shell has long since been modified and improved, but his name and the principle behind his invention survive in the current use of 'shrapnel', which refers to shell fragments of all sorts.

Siege

The laying down of a 'siege' to win the surrender of a city, castle or other fortress is an ancient military tactic dating back to the Siege of Troy and even further. The English 'siege' is derived via the French *assegier* from the Latin *sedere*, meaning 'to sit', which is what a besieging army effectively did. It sat around a fortified position, preventing anyone from escaping or any supplies getting through, and waited until the defenders surrendered.

Since Pontius was a pilot

This RAF euphemism for 'since time immemorial' is a pun on the name of Pontius Pilate, the Roman procurator of Judaea and Samaria at the time of the crucifixion of Jesus Christ.

Skinflint

Anyone who shows excessive meanness, or penny-pinching could be termed a 'skinflint'. The expression originated from the practice of those tight-fisted users of old flintlock guns, who strived to get longer use out of the flints in their guns, rather than simply replacing the worn-out ones with fresh flints. The firing mechanism of the flintlock gun relied on the flint to create a shower of sparks that ignited the small charge of powder in the lockpan which detonated the main charge in the barrel. After a certain amount of use a flint became blunt and therefore less efficient. Those wanting to spare themselves having to get a new flint, sharpened ('skinned') their existing ones with a knife.

Skirmish

'Skirmish' has been used in English since the fourteenth century to describe short-lived engagements between small bodies of fighters. 'Skirmish', along with the sporting expressions 'scrimmage' and 'scrummage', is related to a number of words in several medieval languages to do with swordfights, among them the Italian *scaramuccia*, the Old French *escaramuche*, and the Old German *skirmen*, which means 'to defend'.

Slogan

Today's 'slogan' is a catchphrase devised to draw attention to a product or an individual in search of public recognition. But 'slogan' originally meant a battle-cry raised by Scottish warriors as they charged. The modern spelling of 'slogan' has developed from the Gaelic *sluaghghairm*, in which *sluagh* meant a 'host' and *gairm* a 'shout' or 'cry'.

Smokescreen

A 'smokescreen' is a device intended to deceive others, one that enables the person putting up the 'smokescreen' to hide their real intentions or motives. The allusion is self-evident and recalls the use of smokescreens in naval warfare when small ships, such as destroyers, sailed between the enemy and their own force, belching clouds of black smoke from their engines to conceal the fleet's manoeuvres.

Sniper

The battlefield 'sniper' is a marksman who fires at individual enemy soldiers from a concealed position, which makes him difficult to locate especially in built-up areas, where a skilled sniper can pin down a significant number of enemy troops for some time, before slipping away to set up a new sniping position. Used figuratively, a 'sniper' is one who attacks and criticises covertly. References to 'sniping' and 'snipers' date from the late eighteenth century and appear to allude to a technique for shooting snipe, a long-billed wading birds that are related to the woodcock.

Soldier

The Latin root from which 'soldier' is derived sheds an interesting light on the original nature of soldiering. The Latin word in question is *solidus*, which was a gold coin in use during the time of the Roman Empire. This establishes an early link between 'soldier' and payment, suggesting that early 'soldiers' were indeed 'soldiers of fortune': fighting men who hired themselves for military service.

Son of a gun

Perhaps one of the inevitable consequences of 'showing a leg' was that women about to give birth sometimes found themselves aboard warships. When this happened, a degree of privacy was provided between two guns for their confinement. In cases where the father was unknown, the child (assuming it was a boy) was described as a 'son of a gun'. Since its derivation in the early eighteenth century the expression has shed this specific meaning, becoming instead an inoffensive and light-hearted way of addressing any male individual.

Sortie

'Sortie' is another military term that has found its way directly from French into English. The French noun *sortie*, seen on signs all over the French-speaking world, means 'exit'. In the sense of 'going out', 'sortie' refers to a scouting mission undertaken by a besieged garrison trying to probe enemy lines to reach reinforcements or fresh supplies.

Spearhead

Any person, or group of people, taking the lead in an attack, or any other undertaking in which others will follow, can be said to be both the 'spearhead' itself and to be 'spearheading' the enterprise. The allusion is obviously to the sharpened point of a spear: the 'business' end, made from iron or steel. Spears were used in civilizations at most times and places in history. The

English 'spear' is derived from a number of related Norse and Germanic words; Latin also has the word *sparus* for a 'hunting-spear', but the influence this may have had on the origin of the English word is uncertain.

Spiking his guns

In the early days of field artillery, the charge which propelled the ball or other projectile from the barrel was detonated by igniting its gunpowder through a small touch-hole. If a metal spike was driven in to block this touch-hole, the gun could not be fired and was rendered useless. From this act of battlefield sabotage, 'spiking his guns' has been given a wider application, referring to any action that foils an opponent's plans.

Splicing the mainbrace

In the Royal Navy the order to 'splice the mainbrace' signals the very rare allocation of an extra tot of rum ('grog') to a ship's company. The expression has been used in the Royal Navy since the early years of the nineteenth century and probably originates from the provision of an extra ration of rum to the seamen who succeeded in the difficult and arduous task of splicing (repairing and joining) the 'mainbrace', the rope attached to the yard from which the mainsail hung. Since the days of sailing ships 'splicing the mainbrace' has become a general euphemism for having a drink.

Squad

A 'squad' today might comprise a group of players in a sport's team or a specialist police unit (as in a regional crime 'squad'), as well as a small detachment of soldiers, which was its original meaning. There have been 'squads' of soldiers in the English army since the seventeenth century. Similar details have existed in the armies of other nations and the names for them all share the common root of 'a square formation' in which a 'squad' was traditionally drawn up. In French, for example, *esquade* (dating from the sixteenth century) is a variant of *escadre*, which stems from *écarre*, meaning a 'square'.

Staff officer

A group of officers, not themselves in command, who assist a general or other commanding officer in deploying and supplying an army, or other large military unit, is known as his 'staff'; they themselves are known as 'staff officers'. In this specific military sense, 'staff' originated on the Continent, where it is associated with words like the Dutch *staf* and the German *stab*. The reference here is to the baton carried by officers. An early seventeenth-century writer recorded that in the German army of that time a regiment and everything connected to it was called the 'Colonel's staff', because 'with that the Soldiers are to be ruled'.

Standard-bearer

In the confusion of battle it was important for soldiers to have a rallying point and this often took the form of a tall pole carrying an emblem or banner around which troops could gather and behind which they could launch an attack. The man charged with the task of carrying the standard carried a great responsibility, for if a standard was captured and either disappeared from sight, or was hoisted by the enemy, it could cause panic in his own force. Therefore standard-bearers were invariably brave, dependable warriors, men capable of leading their fellows into battle and maintaining a determined onslaught. 'Standard' originates from the Old French *estendart* which is rooted in the Latin *extendere* ('to stretch out' or 'spread out').

Steal a march on

In its original meaning, to 'steal a march on' an enemy, an army would advance surreptitiously, perhaps moving at night while the enemy slept, thereby surprising them by appearing unexpectedly. A 'march' in this sense was a set distance, one that any army could cover in a given time. The phrase is used by analogy today in the sense of 'gaining an advantage' by acting sooner than expected.

Stentorian

Stentor was the name of a Greek herald at the siege of Troy whose voice, according to Homer, was as loud as the combined voices of fifty men. The adjective 'stentorian' builds on his remarkable ability and since the seventeenth century has been applied to anyone with an abnormally loud voice.

Stiff upper lip

Keeping a 'stiff upper lip' means bearing difficulties and setbacks with fortitude. Today it is used in its figurative sense, but when the expression was first coined in the early days of the Royal Navy, keeping a 'stiff upper lip' was exactly what had to happen. The phrase apparently originated in the tradition of burying the dead at sea. Sailors who died aboard ship, or who were killed in action, were sewn into a weighted shroud and then dropped over the side of the ship. It was customary for the last stitch in the shroud to be passed through the upper lip and lower part of the nose of the corpse. This is a very sensitive part of the body and if any signs of life were to be seen at the final stage of burial preparation, it was believed that a needle pushed through this area of delicate flesh would produce some reaction in even a seemingly lifeless corpse. Sailors trying to escape the Royal Navy by feigning death knew that they would have to endure the agony of this final stitch. Those who succeeded in keeping a 'stiff upper lip' gave away no sign of life and were duly 'buried' at sea. Once in the water, they would be able to cut themselves out of the shroud using a hidden knife and swim to freedom. Clearly one prerequisite of this desperate form of escape was to ensure that your 'burial at sea' took place within swimming distance of the shore.

Strafing

To receive a 'strafing' equates to being given a severe dressing-down, if you are individual, or to come under a sudden, sharp attack if you are caught up in a military conflict. The verb 'strafe' comes from the German *strafen*, meaning 'to punish' and entered English in the twentieth century during the First and Second World Wars, usually with reference to low-level attacks by aircraft machine-gunning enemy positions, vehicles or ships. A German phrase in vogue during the First World War may have had a part to play as well: *Gott strafe England* ('God punish England') was sometimes used as a toast.

Strategy

'Strategy', the planning, controlling and coordinating of resources and personnel, features in a wide variety of contemporary situations: politics, business, industry and sport, as well as defence. For most of its history, though, strategy was the exclusive preserve of military commanders and the word stems from the Greek for a 'general', *strategos*, which literally means in Greek 'the leader of an army'.

Stronghold

In the Middle Ages this was a term applied to a well-fortified position to which those under attack could retire in safety and from which they could defend themselves. Medieval 'strongholds' ranged from small castles to large fortified cities ringed with defensive walls. In this sense a 'stronghold' meant a 'powerful' and, 'vigorous' ('*strong*') 'guard' and 'defence' ('*hold*').

Swashbuckler

The benefit of history has leant the 'swashbuckler' an air of romantic derring-do, aided no doubt by Hollywood, that he might not have expected when the term was coined in the sixteenth century. In those days a 'swashbuckler' was a swaggerer and frequently a ruffian who fancied himself as a swordsman. His unusual name comes from 'swash' meaning 'make a noise like clashing swords' and 'buckler', a small round shield. So, a 'swashbuckler' was a swaggering fellow who banged his sword against his own shield or that of another as a demonstration of his skill with a sword.

Swinging the cat

Until 1881 a nine-lashed scourge called a 'cat-o'-nine-tails' was used against offenders in the British army and the Royal Navy. Aboard ship punishment was exacted on the open deck in the presence of the whole ship's company. Below decks, living conditions were very cramped and it was here that this expression for a 'confined space' developed: down in the crew's quarters there was not enough space to 'swing a cat'.

Swinging the lead

Anyone who concocts a plausible story to avoid work is said to be 'swinging the lead'. The allusion is to the leadsman whose job it was aboard ship to measure the depth of the water through which his ship was sailing. To do this he had to take soundings by throwing a lead weight attached to a line over the side of the ship and noting how much line ran out before the weight touched the bottom. A lazy leadsman could drag this out by idly 'swinging the lead' between soundings.

Tactics

The art of deploying forces in battle has been known as 'tactics', or something very close to it, since ancient times. In Greek, *taktikos* meant 'ordered' and 'arranged'. The word became current in English from the seventeenth century and gradually extended beyond the art of warfare to include other areas in which carefully planned and executed procedures were important in reaching a successful conclusion.

Take by storm

By the seventeenth century 'a storm' meant in English 'an assault of troops' on a place and therefore somewhere 'taken by storm' was a position seized by sudden and overwhelming attack. Used figuratively, the military term has since been applied to anyone who becomes suddenly famous or popular. Performers and stars in other arenas are said to have taken somewhere 'by storm' following a sudden success that has brought them instant fame.

Take down a peg

The metaphorical action of taking someone down a peg is to lower their self-esteem. The expression is generally applied to the conceited and pretentious whose pumped-up egos need deflating. The term originated in the Royal Navy where a ship's colours were raised and lowered by pegs; the higher the colours, the greater the honour, which was diminished if the colours were lowered by being 'taken down a peg'.

Tank

Few battlefield weapons have achieved such a dominant position in warfare as quickly as the 'tank' and few had such an unlikely evolution. The idea of using 'mechanical horses' in battle had been current from the end of the nineteenth century, but the first practical armoured, self-propelled, artillery tractor was designed by the Royal Naval Air Service, encouraged by Winston Churchill, who, as First Lord of the Admiralty, had been impressed by the armoured cars they had used in Flanders in the early days of the First World War. A prototype vehicle was given its first trial in February 1915 and, in spite of a lukewarm reception by the high command, one hundred modified models were commissioned. In order to maintain absolute secrecy, this revolutionary weapon was given a codename. 'Water carrier' was rejected in favour of 'tank' and under this name the first tanks were sent into battle in September 1916. All but eighteen of the forty-nine involved in the action became bogged down, but the eighteen which made it through to the German trenches achieved astonishing results: one captured a village, another a German trench complete with

300 prisoners. When the first full-scale tank assault was launched on the Somme later in the month, 400 tanks spread along a six-mile front led an attack which captured 7,500 prisoners and 120 guns, and pushed deeper into enemy lines than any previous British action. The word 'tank' was an English borrowing of the Indian word *tankh*, which had been known to English residents in India since the seventeenth century as an 'irrigation reservoir' and therefore an artificial receptacle for large quantities of liquids.

Tapping the admiral

This is an expression from days gone by meaning 'to have a surreptitious drink' by broaching a barrel of liquor. It originated from the story (possibly apocryphal) of sailors in the Royal Navy tapping the cask of rum, brandy or other spirit in which the body of a dead admiral was being preserved on its voyage back to England for burial.

Tattoo

Both meanings of 'tattoo' owe their usage in English to the armed services. The elaborate military display known these days as a 'tattoo', originated from the drumbeat which summoned troops back to their barracks at the end of the day. This acquired the name 'tattoo' from the Dutch *taptoe*, meaning 'to put the tap to', in other words to shut the public houses where the troops were drinking. When the term was first used in English in the seventeenth century it was variously known as beating the 'taptoo', 'tapp-too' and 'taptow'. In 1769 Captain James Cook and his crew introduced the other meaning of 'tattoo' into English when he brought one of the few words borrowed from Polynesian to the language. During his Pacific voyages he had encountered Polynesian peoples whose skin was decorated with indelible markings made by puncturing the skin and inserting pigments. These were called *tataus*, which became 'tattow' in eighteenth-century English, before the present-day spelling was adopted.

Tell it to the Marines

A far-fetched story that raises doubts in the mind of a listener is open to the rejoinder 'tell it to the Marines'; a phrase that is said to have originated from a conversation between Samuel Pepys and Charles II. Pepys, who rose through the civil service to become secretary to the Admiralty, was regaling the King with stories gathered from sailors and mentioned flying fish. Courtiers hearing his description of them scoffed at the notion, but an officer of the Maritime Regiment of Foot confirmed their existence from his own observation. This endorsement was good enough for the King who said, 'From the very nature of their calling no class of our subjects can have so wide a knowledge of seas and lands as the officers and men of Our Loyal Maritime regiment. Henceforward ere ever we cast doubts upon a tale that lacks likelihood we will first "Tell it to the Marines".'

The die is cast

When 'the die is cast' the step has been taken from which there is no turning back. The phrase dates from 49 B.C. when Julius Caesar led his army across the Rubicon, thereby beginning a civil war against Pompey and the Roman Senate. His comment at the time was spoken in Greek, but it has often been quoted in Latin as *jacta alea est!* ('the die has been cast'). In the Latin sentence the word for 'die' is *alea*, but the English word 'die' originates from a different Latin word: *dare* meaning 'to give'.

Three sheets in the wind

This colourful naval expression for being very drunk dates from the days of sailing ships when the sails were trimmed and set in their correct positions by means of ropes, known aboard ship as 'sheets'. A 'sheet' which had come loose allowing part of the sail to flap freely was said to be 'in the wind'. To be 'a sheet in the wind' is a naval expression for being tiddly, so to be 'three sheets in the wind' and thereby seriously out of control, was to be very drunk indeed.

Throwing down the gauntlet

Presenting a challenge to someone else can be termed as 'throwing down the gauntlet', a phrase that makes figurative use of a medieval custom in which a challenger removed the metal-plated glove of his armour and threw it to the ground. If the other person accepted the challenge, custom dictated that he showed this by picking up the gauntlet. Given the construction and weight of a medieval 'gauntlet' it is surprising to find that the word is actually a diminutive of the French for a 'glove' (*gant*), which renders the Old French *gantelet* (from which the English is derived) as 'little glove'.

Too much of the bow-hand

Failure brought about by a lack of dexterity can be put down to 'too much of the bow-hand', a phrase which recalls the expertise (or possible lack of it) of the medieval archer. The bow-hand in this case was the left hand, the hand which, in a right-hand dominated world, is invariably associated with clumsiness, as the expression 'cack-handed'. With 'too much of the bow-hand', the left hand takes the blame both for its influence in producing a poor shot from the bow itself, as well as for any other function which fails from a lack of skill and adroitness.

Top brass

In any organization today the 'top brass' are the most senior officers or executives. In the British armed forces at the end of the nineteenth century the term applied to the highest ranking generals and admirals, the brims of whose caps bore gold oak leaves. They became known as 'brass hats' as well as 'the top brass', but it is this last meaning which had been taken up in other walks of life by the beginning of the Second World War.

Torpedo

In 1866 Robert Whitehead, manager of an engineering firm at Fiume on the Adriatic developed a new naval weapon. This was similar in conception to the medieval fireship, but introduced a far more sophisticated and accurate addition to the naval arsenal. His first 'torpedo' was a small, self-propelled boat, stuffed with explosives and steered on the surface by wires. Within two years he was making torpedoes in the now familiar shape of long cylinders. These were powered by compressed air and could carry an explosive charge of 20lb (9kg) at a speed of 7 knots (subsequently improved to 29 knots); later refinements included gyroscopic controls. In principle, all the components of the modern torpedo were in place in the last quarter of the nineteenth century. The device got its name from a type of flat fish of the genus Torpedo, which emits electric charges. The term had earlier been applied to cases filled with gunpowder that were designed to explode underwater, but it was Whitehead who developed the self-propelled submarine missile to which the name 'torpedo' is given today.

Trojan horse

A 'Trojan horse' these days is a 'deception' or 'concealed danger', deriving from the ancient story of the wooden horse used by the Greek army finally to gain entry to the city of Troy after the siege lasting ten years.

Trooper

The Covenanting Army raised in Scotland in 1640 was the first to apply the term 'trooper' to a cavalry soldier and this distinction between a mounted soldier and a foot soldier has lasted ever since. The term 'troop' has been applied to a body of soldiers (and a number of civilians gathered together for that matter) since the sixteenth century; its origin being French and German-based words for a 'herd', such as the French *troupeau*. Despite soldiers of all branches of the army sharing common predilections and no doubt being indistinguishable in their behaviour, the 'trooper' has been branded for some reason as the whipping-boy for all soldierly excesses. So expressions like 'to lie like a trooper' and 'to eat like a trooper' entered the language. Another one in use today is 'to swear like a trooper'.

Trophy

The 'trophy' awarded to the winner of any event or competition harks back to the spoils of battle in the ancient world. Both Latin and Greek have words similar to 'trophy' which described the display of captured arms and standards that was erected after a battle to serve as a memorial to the victory. These words stemmed from the Greek *trope*, meaning 'turning', 'putting to flight' and 'defeating'. By the sixteenth century 'trophy' had acquired its wider meaning in English as an 'award' or 'honour' for any victory.

Turncoat

A 'turncoat' is a renegade; one who deserts his principles or associates to save himself or further his own ends. Legend holds that the term originated with a sometime Duke of Saxony, whose lands were bordered by French territory. Self-interest determined that he kept in with both his Saxon subjects and his French neighbours, so he took to wearing a reversible coat with one side coloured Saxon blue and the other French white. When he wanted to be seen supporting Saxon interests, he wore his coat blue-side out; when it was prudent to show favour towards the French, the coat was turned and he wore it white-side out.

Turning a blind eye

This famous euphemism for 'deliberately overlooking' something dates from the Battle of Copenhagen fought on 2 April 1801. Nelson, second in command of the British fleet sent to the Baltic, was frustrated by the delay of Sir Hyde Parker when the fleet under his command laid siege to Copenhagen. Nelson decided to attack with the ships under his command, ignoring signals flags from the flagship that he should withdraw. When the signal was pointed out to him, Nelson raised his telescope to the eye that had been blinded at Calvi and replied that he could not see any signal. 'I have only one eye,' he told his officers, 'I have a right to be blind sometimes: I really do not see the signal'.

Tyro

A beginner or novice in any undertaking has been called a 'tyro' in English since the seventeenth century. Originally spelt 'tiro', it is a direct borrowing of the Latin word *tiro* which was applied to a young soldier or recruit in the Roman army. In medieval Latin the 'i' became a 'y', creating the word which is still in use today.

Undermining

The modern meaning of 'undermine', to weaken gradually and by subterfuge, comes from medieval siege-craft. The term appeared in English in the fourteenth century when it was common practice for besiegers to tunnel underneath walls and other fortifications, either to weaken them or to gain entry. The tunnels they dug were known as 'mines'. This term had been current in English a century earlier for underground workings from which minerals and ores were extracted; 'mine' was derived from an earlier Celtic word for 'ore'.

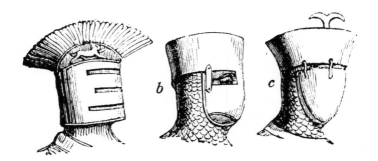

Veni, vidi, vici

Translated into English as 'I came, I saw, I conquered', these three Latin words were used by Julius Caesar as a terse summary of his Pontic campaign which concluded with his victory at the Battle of Zela, in north-eastern Asia Minor, in 47 B.C. Since then they have been used, ironically in many cases, to denote other triumphs.

V.I.P.

The use of these initials, standing for 'Very Important Person', was first coined in 1944 by a station commander of Transport Command who had the responsibility of arranging a flight to the Middle East for Lord Mountbatten and several other important individuals. In order to avoid revealing the identity of the passengers, he referred to them in the plane's orders as 'V.I.P.s'.

Visor

By the fourteenth century the armour worn in battle by many European fighters included a movable covering attached to the helmet that could be positioned to cover the wearer's face. This faceguard was called a 'visor' after *vis*, the French for 'face'. In the twentieth century 'visor' was applied to movable sunshields fitted to the front screens of cars and aircraft.

Ward room

In ships of the Royal Navy the 'ward room' has been the mess used by the ship's officers since the term was first coined in the eighteenth century. It derives from the 'ward robe', the compartment on board which was used to store booty captured from prize ships. From providing accommodation to officers, the 'ward room' gradually became a term by which the ship's officers above the rank of lieutenant were themselves known.

Washout

A 'washout' was slang used by both the army and navy. In the Royal Navy a 'washout' was a 'cancellation', that originated from naval signalling. At one time it was standard practice to record received messages by writing them on a slate. When they were no longer needed, the slate was wiped clean and the message became a 'washout'. In the army, 'washouts' occurred on the shooting range where shots that were way off target were covered over with a coat of paint or 'wash' when the old iron targets were refurbished.

Watchword

In its original meaning a 'watchword' was a password given to sentries in order to gain admission to wherever they were on guard; 'watch' in this sense being derived from the Old English *waeccan* ('to be awake'). This sense of common purpose resulted in the derivation of the modern meaning of 'watchword', as a slogan or phrase that epitomizes a commonly held principle.

Waterloo

The Battle of Waterloo fought on 18 June 1815 was the last battle fought by Napoleon Bonaparte, who led 72,000 French troops against an allied force of 68,000 British, Belgian, Dutch and German troops under the command of the Duke of Wellington. After fighting for much of the day, the allies finally secured their celebrated victory with the intervention of the Prussian force led by Blücher. Unable to raise another army, Napoleon was forced to surrender and was exiled to the mid-Atlantic island of St Helena, where he died in 1821. Since then 'Waterloo' has been used to mean a 'final conflict' or 'crushing defeat'.

Weathering the storm

In the days of sailing ships, when the wind was the only motive power, storms were even more alarming and hazardous than they are to modern vessels. The high winds accompanying storms threatened to tear a ship's sails to threads if they were left fully exposed to the elements. However, reducing the sail-area meant reducing the control the crew had over the direction of the ship's passage, which brought further risks of being blown aground when they were sailing close to the shore. Even if they avoided shipwreck, a storm could blow a sailing vessel far off-course. Therefore those ships and crews that survived a storm were said to have 'weathered' it. ('Weather' in earlier usage had a specific reference to the wind, as in the case of a 'weathercock' which indicates wind direction). In modern usage, 'weathering a storm' is applied figuratively to surviving any turbulent period of stress, trouble and anxiety.

Wellington boots

The name of the first Duke of Wellington, has been applied to a range of objects and institutions from an English public school to a Second World War bomber. However, he is most widely remembered for 'wellington boots', a style of footwear which he popularized during the Napoleonic wars. The first 'wellington boots' were riding boots, in which the top reached above the knee in the front. This was followed by a mid-calf-length boot, sometimes worn under trousers, which was called a 'half-Wellington'. In the early twentieth century the first waterproof 'wellington' appeared, made from specially treated leather. This was followed by the rubber 'wellington boot' which in due course was joined by the plastic 'wellington'.

Whining

The whinging sound of querulous complaint that is 'whining' today is a far cry from the medieval battlefield where 'whining' was first heard. The closest that modern usage comes to the original meaning is in the sense of 'whining' bullets. When 'whining' came into being it was applied to the droning sound of the flight an arrow, which in early English was termed *hwinan*. The change of spelling which transposed the first two letters to produce 'whine' came about through the process of metathesis that altered the spellings of many English words to arrive at their modern versions.

With flying colours

Victorious warships signal their triumphs at sea by returning to port with all their flags ('colours') still flying. Therefore, by analogy, anything that is accomplished 'with flying colours' can be regarded as a total triumph.

Women and children first

The jocular use to which this phrase is used in many circumstances when people have to make their way through a confined space masks the tragedy behind its origin in a mid-nineteenth-century shipwreck. In 1852 HMS *Birkenhead*, en route for South Africa with a force of 476 British soldiers, ran aground fifty miles off the Cape of Good Hope. Only three of the eight lifeboats could be launched and these were soon filled by the twenty women and children who were also on board. As the ship went down, the troops mustered on deck calmly stood their ground. Since then 'women and children first' has been known in the Royal Navy as the Birkenhead Drill.

Your number is up

This was another naval euphemism for death, alluding to the loss of a mess number when a sailor was killed.

Zeroing in on

Aiming at targets became more accurate in the Second World War, due in part to improvements in calibrated gun-sights. Fine adjustment increased the chances of hitting a target and 'zeroing in on' an objective or goal has become a widely-used expression for focusing attention on a particular person or goal.